POP CULTURE

American Life and Celebrity Icons from Marilyn Monroe to Taylor Swift

CATHLEEN SMALL

Cavendish Square
New York

Published in 2017 by Cavendish Square Publishing, LLC
243 5th Avenue, Suite 136, New York, NY 10016

First Edition

Website: cavendishsq.com

CPSIA Compliance Information: Batch #CS16CSQ

All websites were available and accurate when this book was sent to press.

Cataloging-in-Publication Data

Names: Small, Cathleen.
Title: American life and celebrity icons from Marilyn Monroe to Taylor Swift / Cathleen Small.
Description: New York : Cavendish Square, 2017. | Series: Pop culture | Includes index.
Identifiers: ISBN 9781502619792 (library bound) | ISBN 9781502619808 (ebook)
Subjects: LCSH: Celebrities--Juvenile literature. | Popular culture--United States--Juvenile literature.
Classification: LCC HM621.S63 2017 | DDC 306--dc23

Editorial Director: David McNamara
Editor: Kelly Spence
Copy Editor: Nathan Heidelberger
Art Director: Jeffrey Talbot
Designer: Jessica Nevins
Production Assistant: Karol Szymczuk
Photo Research: J8 Media

The photographs in this book are used by permission and through the courtesy of: Keystone Features/Getty Images, cover (background); Steve Granitz/WireImage/Getty Images, cover; Central Press/Getty Images, 4; J. Howard Miller/File:We Can Do It!.jpg/Wikimedia Commons, 6; Silver Screen Collection/Hulton Archive/Getty Images, 10; Alfred Eisenstaedt/The LIFE Picture Collection/Getty Images, 12; Darlene Hammond/Hulton Archive/Getty Images, 14; AGIP/RDA/Getty Images, 17; Michael Ochs Archives/Getty Images, 19; Frank Hurley/NY Daily News Archive via Getty Images, 25; ullstein bild/ullstein bild via Getty Images, 29; Michael Webb/Getty Images, 31; David Redfern/Redferns/Getty Images, 35; Marion S. Trikosko, U.S. News & World Report Magazine/File:MLK and Malcolm X USNWR cropped.jpg/Wikimedia Commons, 37; Harry Dempster/Daily Express/Hulton Archive/Getty Images, 41; Michael Ochs Archives/Getty Images, 43; Movie Poster Image Art/Getty Images, 45; Terry O'Neill/Getty Images, 47; Hulton Archive/Getty Images, 49; MTV/File:Mtvmoon.png/Wikimedia Commons, 52; Ron Galella/WireImage, 57; The LIFE Picture Collection/Getty Images, 59; Harry Langdon/Getty Images, 63; AP Photo/Richard Drew, 65; Diana Walker/Time Life Pictures/Getty Images, 68; Karl Gehring/Liaison/Getty Images, 73; Michel Linssen/Redferns/Getty Images, 74; Rob Verhorst/Redferns/Getty Images, 77; Julie Alissi/J8 Media, 79; Michael Smith/Hulton Archive/Getty Images, 84; Kevin Mazur/Getty Images for Yeezy Season 3, 87; 7831/Gamma-Rapho via Getty Images, 89; DFree/Shutterstock.com, 91; Jon Kopaloff/FilmMagic/Getty Images, 93.

Printed in the United States of America

Contents

Reverend Martin Luther King Jr., an icon of the 1960s civil rights movement, gave his famous "I Have a Dream" speech from the steps of the Lincoln Memorial in Washington, DC.

Introduction

POPULAR CULTURE IS THE DOMINANT IDEAS of a specific culture at a given time. The goings-on in the world during any given time period are reflected in the movies, books, television shows, mass media, and slang of the era. Certain personalities emerge from popular culture and stand out as icons. They may be specific representatives of something important going on at the time, such as a president during a time of war, or they may simply be personalities who inspire hope, happiness, or fascination in the American public at a time when they are much needed.

These pop culture icons can have a lasting influence on society. For example, strong females in the media have had a tremendous effect on the **feminist** movement, and powerful African-American figures advanced **civil rights**. Other individuals simply capture the attention of Americans through challenging societal norms, or through scandal and intrigue.

Together, pop culture and society are inextricably linked, and the icons that emerge from each decade are solid representations of that link.

The image of tough-girl Rosie the Riveter symbolized the women who worked in factories and shipyards during World War II.

ONE

1950s: Living the Dream

AMERICA CAME INTO THE 1950S ON THE heels of the turbulence of World War II (1939–1945). The conflict had ended in 1945, but the latter years of the decade were a time of rebuilding and reestablishing relationships. Men who had gone off to war returned home and had to readjust to the family life they had left behind. Men who didn't return left families struggling to rebuild their lives. And men weren't the only ones who had to readjust. Women had played an active role in the war as well, both on the home front and overseas. At home, they took on roles that men had previously held and began to work outside of the home, filling positions that had been vacated by the soldiers going across the pond to fight. Women actively participated in the war effort overseas as well, working in military reserves and auxiliary corps and as nurses.

It was quite an adjustment when the war ended, and people had to redefine their personal and professional roles. Many women wanted to continue working, but the job market wasn't particularly welcoming—it seemed that if men were available to do a job, then men were preferred. Books, television shows, movies, and even advertisements encouraged women to get back into the home and back to the business of raising a family and creating a home for their husbands.

Having had a taste of the working world, many women struggled to transition back into the role of homemaker. At the same time, men struggled to accept that women were becoming interested in taking on roles outside the home. There were, of course, women who welcomed the shift back to a traditional household and homemaker role, but many women liked the sense of independence that the war had given them.

It was a time of change, for sure, but by the time the 1950s rolled around, an uneasy dynamic was in place. Middle-class families were moving out of cities and into the **suburbs**. Iconic television shows of the time, such as *Father Knows Best* (1954–1960) and *Leave It to Beaver* (1957–1963), portrayed the ideal all-American family: a father who went off to work every day, a sweet, maternal mother who stayed home to raise a family, and a couple of impish but well-meaning children.

Whether husbands and wives were happy in these roles depends, of course, on individual people. But for better or for worse, this was the family dynamic that existed in the 1950s. Some women may have yearned for the freedom they had during the war years, but society wasn't ready to support that yet, so they largely returned to their roles in the home. And so the American Dream of a house in the suburbs, a father, a mother, and a couple of children dominated the decade.

THE ICONIC BLONDES

In this version of the American Dream, mothers were usually neatly clothed in dresses that accentuated their figures pleasingly, and their blonde hair was carefully coifed. Of course, not every woman was a blonde—but the image of the iconic blonde beauty was a 1950s ideal, and several popular actresses of the time fit that image.

THE MODERN PRINCESS

One of the best-known iconic blondes of the decade was Grace Kelly. With her fresh good looks, perfectly styled blonde hair, and wholesome appearance, she captured the hearts of America in films such as *Dial M for Murder* (1954) and *Rear Window* (1954), starring alongside leading men like Cary Grant and Frank Sinatra.

But what *really* vaulted Grace Kelly into icon status was her 1956 marriage to Monaco's Prince Rainier III. It proved that every little girl's dream could come true—you really *could* grow up to fall in love and marry a prince!

The reality may have been slightly less romantic. It was well known that Prince Rainier was actively seeking a wife when he met with Kelly in late 1955. He proposed three days later, at which point she had to provide a $2 million **dowry** for the marriage. However, she had been corresponding with Prince Rainier for months before the meeting and seemed to embrace giving up her acting career in favor of royal duties in Monaco. She went on to have three children with Prince Rainier and remained married to him until her death in a car accident in 1982. Prince Rainier never remarried after his wife's death.

Seventy years after her marriage to a prince, Grace Kelly remains an icon. The television series *Mad Men*, set in the 1960s, depicts a 1950s domestic model in which the main character's wife, Betty Draper, considered a trophy as far as wives go, is a dead ringer for Grace Kelly.

THE BLONDE BOMBSHELL

While Grace Kelly appeared to be the wholesome princess, another 1950s blonde embodied a much different **persona**: the **bombshell**. That blonde was Norma Jeane Mortenson, better known as Marilyn Monroe.

In reality, Grace Kelly wasn't necessarily as wholesome of a princess as the studios wanted moviegoers to believe. There are reports of her having relationships with her costars—regardless of their marital status. This certainly would have been frowned upon in the conservative 1950s. But movie studios and the press are powerful entities when it comes to crafting a persona, and they created an image of Grace Kelly as the girl next door who went on to marry a prince.

But with Marilyn Monroe, the persona that made her famous was that of a ditzy blonde sex symbol. Indeed, she started her career as a pinup model before making the jump to the big screen, where she generally played the role of an attractive but not very bright blonde. The public loved the blonde bombshell—largely for her unapologetic sex appeal.

Monroe's troubled personal life didn't do anything to alter her image, either. She was married three times, and all three ended in divorce. Two of the marriages were very public: to baseball icon Joe DiMaggio and to playwright Arthur Miller. Her struggles with depression and addiction were no secret, and it is widely believed that Monroe had an affair with then-President John F. Kennedy, too.

Marilyn Monroe was likely nowhere near as ditzy as her public image indicated. She'd survived a tough childhood in foster care and an early, unfulfilling marriage. During

Opposite: The iconic blonde-turned-princess, Grace Kelly

World War II, she was one of many women who took to the workforce. By all reports, Monroe took her work as a model and an actress seriously and was eager to do well in both. She had an ambition that would likely be lacking if she was truly the "dumb blonde" that she was made out to be.

But Monroe knew what it took for success, and she played up her assets accordingly. Her clothes accentuated her curvy figure, and she spoke in a soft, breathy voice that fit the sex symbol she was portrayed to be. When Monroe died at the young age of thirty-six, she went from icon to legend—particularly given the swirling rumors and **conspiracy theories** surrounding her death. She was a bombshell who was clearly a lot more complicated than anyone ever knew—or gave her credit for.

A FEUD AMONG ICONS

Yet another blonde icon of the 1950s was the wholesome and multitalented actress, singer, and dancer Debbie Reynolds. In the 1950s, she was a major movie star, and her success continued throughout the 1960s and beyond. America's Sweetheart became even sweeter when she married singer Eddie Fisher in 1955, although some believe the marriage was more for publicity than for true love. They had two children, one of whom went on to become a celebrity icon in her own right: Carrie Fisher, of Star Wars fame.

Unfortunately, Reynolds's picture-perfect marriage wouldn't last long. Another iconic actress of the time, Elizabeth Taylor, was good friends with the couple. Taylor was an exception to the iconic blonde actresses of the 1950s;

Opposite: Women still imitate the iconic look of Marilyn Monroe today.

Friends for a time: Elizabeth Taylor (*left*), shown with then-husband Mike Todd, would go on to bewitch Debbie Reynolds's (*right*) husband, Eddie Fisher.

with her raven hair, lavender eyes, and porcelain skin, she was an exotic, captivating beauty. And indeed, when her husband of one year, Mike Todd, was killed in a plane crash, Taylor managed to captivate Eddie Fisher—and steal him away from Debbie Reynolds.

Although Taylor was painted as a home wrecker for breaking up the young marriage—and Debbie Reynolds did nothing to dispel that notion—the two women later settled their feud and rekindled their friendship. In 2010,

Reynolds reflected on the situation, saying, "I understand when I look back on it. Who would pass by Elizabeth? No woman living was as beautiful as her." And anyway, Reynolds's prediction for her husband came true: Taylor had already been married three times when Fisher declared he wanted a divorce from Reynolds, who told him, "She will throw you

The Red Scare and Everyone's Favorite Redhead

Among a sea of blondes and the occasional brunette, another actress and comedian stands out as an icon: the inimitable Lucille Ball. She and her husband, Cuban-born Desi Arnaz, were the stars of the wildly popular 1950s sitcom *I Love Lucy*. All was well and good with America's redheaded sweetheart until 1953, when the House Un-American Activities Committee (HUAC) publicly reported that Ball had registered as a member of the **Communist** Party in the 1930s. In the late 1940s, HUAC began investigating various influential Hollywood people to determine whether they had communist ties—part of the so-called Red Scare.

The HUAC investigations resulted in many artists being **blacklisted**, including Charlie Chaplin, Orson Welles, and Dalton Trumbo. This blacklisting destroyed the careers of many Hollywood artists, though a few were able to rebuild their careers. Unsinkable redhead Lucille Ball weathered the scandal and emerged relatively unscathed. Ball provided twenty-seven pages of testimony indicating that although she had registered as a member of the Communist Party, she had never voted for the party and wasn't an active member. She claimed she had registered for the party to appease her grandfather, who was an outspoken socialist. HUAC and FBI Director J. Edgar Hoover, who was apparently a big fan of *I Love Lucy*, cleared Ball's name.

out within eighteen months." And indeed, Taylor fell in love with Richard Burton on the set of *Cleopatra* in 1962 and divorced Fisher for Burton two years later.

THE LEADING MEN

The leading ladies of the 1950s needed leading men, and indeed, several became iconic. Early in the 1950s, Marlon Brando shot to fame for his portrayal of Stanley Kowalski in *A Streetcar Named Desire* (1951). He went on to further success in *On the Waterfront* (1954), for which he won an Academy Award, and later *The Godfather* (1972), for which he won his second Academy Award. Brando tended to play dark, brooding, or rebellious characters, which made the attractive young actor all the more appealing to women drawn to his "bad boy" persona. And indeed, Brando's drama-filled personal life in some ways seemed to mirror his art. Brando ultimately fathered at least sixteen children from numerous wives and girlfriends. One of his many relationships, according to his autobiography, was with another icon on the time: none other than Marilyn Monroe!

Another iconic leading man of the 1950s was pretty much the polar opposite of Brando: Paul Newman. With his boyish good looks and sparkling blue eyes, Newman captured the hearts of American women in part for his acting work and in part due to his fifty-year marriage to fellow actress Joanne Woodward, which lasted until his death in 2008.

Despite a lifelong struggle with alcoholism, Newman was a hugely successful actor in numerous stage plays and films, including *Cat on a Hot Tin Roof* (1958), starring the

Opposite: **Paul Newman, circa 1960.**

iconic Elizabeth Taylor; *The Hustler* (1961); and *The Color of Money* (1986), which earned him an Academy Award for Best Actor. But he wasn't content to just act. Newman had a love of auto racing, and he indulged that love starting in 1972, when he entered his first race as a driver. He continued to race cars until 2007, when he retired from professional racing at the age of eighty-two. Newman was also a well-known **philanthropist**. His Newman's Own line of food products, which he cofounded with author A. E. Hotchner, was quite successful, and Newman ensured that all proceeds from the company after taxes would be donated to charity. As of 2014, the company had donated more than $400 million to charity. In addition, in 1988 Newman cofounded a summer camp for seriously ill children, which he named the Hole in the Wall Gang Camp; the name was a tribute to his 1969 film *Butch Cassidy and the Sundance Kid*, which featured a gang of the same name.

Still, many leading men of the 1950s, like the leading women, were much more complicated than the press and studios portrayed them to be. Reality was whitewashed to sell an image that gelled with the American Dream.

MUSICAL ICONS OF THE 1950S

Certainly actors and actresses weren't the only icons of the decade. Whereas 1940s music had been mostly of the swing and big band style, pop and rock became king in the 1950s. As happens with pretty much every era, parents shook their heads in dismay at the "new music," thinking it somewhat

Opposite: Many people consider Elvis Presley to be the king of rock and roll. Some of his most-loved songs include a 1956 cover of "Hound Dog" and 1957's "All Shook Up" and "Jailhouse Rock."

scandalous. So, of course, teenagers loved the upbeat new sounds of pop and rock.

In an era of new music and new artists, one stands out in the American music scene: a young man from Tupelo, Mississippi, named Elvis Presley. His rock songs incorporated elements of country and rhythm and blues, in an early rockabilly style.

Elvis's rock sound and suggestive performance style made him quite controversial. Many parents thought his music was too suggestive for their children—he shocked conservative audiences when he appeared on *The Milton Berle Show* and sang his hit song "Hound Dog" while doing his signature "pelvis shaking." (This earned him the nickname of "Elvis the Pelvis.") Conservative and religious groups declared his performance vulgar and warned parents against allowing their children to listen to his music. So scandalized was the public by Elvis's dance moves that for one of his appearances on the family-oriented *The Ed Sullivan Show*, the singer was shot only from the waist up.

Controversy can help make an icon, and it certainly didn't hurt in Elvis's case. He had it all: dark good looks, a singing style that electrified young audiences, and a certain bad-boy charm that piqued people's interest, even while others raised their eyebrows. Underneath it all, Elvis was reportedly devoted to his family and loyal to his spiritual roots. After serving in the US Army, Elvis returned to singing and moved into acting as well. Although his movies weren't a critical success, the public enjoyed them, and they were profitable, further cementing Presley as an American icon. His iconic status changed to legendary when he died at the young age of forty-two.

GONE TOO SOON

Some icons are part of American culture for decades, but others have flames that are extinguished far too quickly—and indeed, their premature deaths are likely part of what cements them as icons.

One such icon was James Dean, an American actor who died at the young age of twenty-four. Dean only made three films before his death—*Rebel Without a Cause* (1955), *East of Eden* (1955), and the posthumously released *Giant* (1956)—but those three films were enough to cement him as *the* iconic rebel without a cause in American culture.

In all three films, Dean played a troubled or disillusioned loner. Dean's troubled personal life mirrored the isolated characters he played in his films. Many women were drawn to the actor's "bad boy" image. Perhaps his rebellious attitude was a refreshing change for the 1950s housewives, who longed for something different from a husband who came home every day from a nine-to-five job and wanted a hot meal waiting on the table. Whatever the reason, James Dean was a hit. Like Elvis, he went from icon to legend when he died tragically in a car accident in 1955.

Also gone far too soon and thusly turned into icons were three musicians who had been making their names in the American music scene when their small plane crashed in 1959, killing all three. Buddy Holly, Ritchie Valens, and the Big Bopper (aka J. P. Richardson) left an Iowa airport and headed for their next show in North Dakota in a small plane that Holly had chartered. The plane crashed in a snowstorm, and America mourned the lost lives and talent. The Big Bopper, known for his hit song "Chantilly Lace" (1958), was the oldest of the three, at age twenty-eight. Buddy Holly, at age twenty-two, had already scored a number of hits, including "Peggy Sue" and "That'll Be the Day" in 1957, and had opened for the iconic Elvis Presley in concert. Ritchie Valens, the baby of the three at age seventeen, was rapidly gaining fame in the American-Chicano rock movement for his hit "La Bamba" (1958).

The plane crash was later referred to as "the day the music died," and it was immortalized in Don McLean's famous 1972 hit "American Pie"—a song that the Recording Industry Association of America considers to be among the top five songs of the twentieth century.

DECADE IN REVIEW

On the surface, the 1950s were the decade of the American Dream. The war was over, the men were home, and the women were settled back into their role as homemakers. But there was an unsettled undercurrent running through the decade. Women were restless. Men were restless. And through it all, the fear of communism lay like a silent threat. It wasn't the idyllic decade that it appeared to be.

TWO

1960s: War and Counterculture

AFTER THE SEEMINGLY IDYLLIC 1950S, WITH its picture-perfect surface and it's subtle, hidden unrest, America moved into the turbulent 1960s, a decade of war and unease.

When John F. Kennedy took the oath of office in 1961, he became America's youngest elected president. He and his beautiful young wife, Jackie, ushered in an idealistic era of hope and prosperity that was later referred to as Camelot. The 1960 musical *Camelot* was a favorite of the president and his wife, and Jackie quoted a favorite line in a *Life* interview given after her husband's assassination, saying: "Don't let it be forgot, that once there was a spot, for one brief shining moment that was Camelot ... There'll be great presidents again, but there'll never be another Camelot again."

But this Camelot era wasn't as glittering and polished as it seemed. The young president faced the Cuban missile crisis, a tense two-week period in which Kennedy negotiated with Soviet leader Nikita Khrushchev to remove the Soviet missiles that had been placed in Cuba and put the United States in range for the threat of devastating nuclear war.

Meanwhile, the conflict in Vietnam (largely known as the Vietnam War, although technically, it was never declared a war by Congress—only a conflict) continued to escalate. The war was between North and South Vietnam. However, the United States was intricately involved as they supported South Vietnam's attempts to remain independent from communist North Vietnam. As the decade progressed, the United States became increasingly involved, sending more and more troops over—which, naturally, resulted in more and more American casualties. Further, **photojournalism** and video technology had become widely used, which meant that the Vietnam Conflict was playing out in newspapers and on television sets across the country. For the first time, people could see nearly firsthand the ravages and brutality of war—and they did *not* like it. In fact, the conflict was wildly unpopular with a large segment of the American public, who felt that American soldiers were fighting in and dying for a war that they had no place in. The public also felt that the government was whitewashing the Vietnam Conflict and giving them a sanitized version of the events occurring in Southeast Asia. The images they saw in the media didn't match with what politicians were telling them about supposed successes in the war, and the public began to be increasingly distrustful of the government.

Despite the unpopularity of the war and the growing public mistrust of the government, Kennedy remained a popular president. The American public was devastated when he was assassinated in November 1963, at the age of forty-six. As Jackie Kennedy had said, the era of Camelot was over.

THE QUEEN OF CAMELOT

Not only was John F. Kennedy a popular president; his attractive wife Jackie was a fashion icon. In fact, *Harper's*

Presidential nominee John F. Kennedy and his wife, Jackie—iconic figures of the early 1960s.

Bazaar described her as "one of the greatest style icons of the last century." America may have lacked a royal family, but Jackie certainly made up for its lack of a queen. Her regal beauty and style were admired by women who watched to see what fashion-forward styles Jackie would wear next. Part of her signature look were the pillbox hat, designed for her by Halston, and oversized black sunglasses. She was a big fan of American designer Oleg Cassini, but she also enjoyed wearing clothing by French designers Christian Dior, Balenciaga, and Givenchy. First Ladies have always been in the public eye, but Jackie Kennedy's elegance, beauty, and style made her an iconic First Lady like none before her. Half a century later, her fashion sense still inspires modern designs.

GIVE PEACE A CHANCE

Amid the atmosphere of death and deception, young people looked for beacons of peace, hope, and love. They found it in the **hippie** culture that sprang up in San Francisco and New York City and quickly spread to other regions as well.

The hippies were a part of the **counterculture**, which basically pushed back against the established values and systems of the 1950s. Members of the counterculture wanted freedom and acceptance for all—they embraced women's rights and minority rights, and they pushed against the established **patriarchy** of the 1950s and the strict sexual conventions of the time. They felt that people should be free to love one another and explore their true selves, rather than conforming to what "the establishment" dictated. Part of this era of expression involved experimenting with drugs and sexuality.

So the 1960s began as a decade of free love, drug use, nonconformity, and recognition and acceptance of alternative cultures and lifestyles. The counterculture/hippie era was proudly and loudly represented by the musical icons of the era, which included folk, rock, and Motown artists.

MOTOWN AND ACCEPTANCE

At first glance, Motown might not *seem* like part of the counterculture movement. When we think of hippies, we think of flower children and Woodstock, not necessarily of African-American artists. But the counterculture era took place during the civil rights movement, and the two were inextricably linked. Members of the counterculture supported civil rights and Martin Luther King Jr.'s quest for equality for African Americans.

Motown figured prominently at this time because it welcomed black artists into mainstream music. Motown artists such as Stevie Wonder and Diana Ross certainly had their appeal to the African-American community, but they had crossover appeal to white audiences as well. Whereas conservative, largely Caucasian audiences of the 1950s had decried Elvis's music as being "too black," in the more relaxed atmosphere of the 1960s, more white audiences began to appreciate the talent and style of black artists.

Perhaps the most iconic of the Motown artists were the Jackson 5, a group of African-American brothers from Gary, Indiana. They were a late addition to the Motown record label in 1969, but they gained wide appeal. The group followed the crossover path paved by earlier Motown artists like the Supremes (headed by Diana Ross), the Four Tops, and the Temptations. The Jackson 5 scored seventeen Top 40 singles and were successful as a group, but they became iconic in retrospect, after one of the brothers, Michael, became a phenomenally successful solo artist in the 1980s.

MAKE LOVE, NOT WAR

The counterculture of the 1960s was firmly antiwar, and one iconic voice of this generation was Bob Dylan, a folk singer-songwriter whose songs "Blowin' in the Wind" (1963) and "The Times They Are a-Changin'" (1965) became symbolic of the antiwar movement in the United States. Further supporting the peace-loving counterculture movement was a duo known as Simon & Garfunkel, who experienced wild success and popular acclaim with the release of four albums in the late 1960s before breaking up in 1970.

For those who felt the United States was fighting in a war where it didn't belong, the gentle, peace-loving songs of the counterculture artists were a welcome haven. Their peaceful melodies and powerful lyrics became anthems for a generation desiring peace and acceptance. As Dylan's "Blowin' in the Wind" asks:

> How many times must the cannonballs fly
> Before they're forever banned? ...
>
> How many times can some people exist
> Before they're allowed to be free?
>
> The answer, my friend, is blowing in the wind
> The answer is blowing in the wind

THE BRITISH INVASION

Counterculture wasn't solely an American construct, though. It was forever changed by the arrival of four young men from England informally known as the Fab Four—and better known as the Beatles.

Bob Dylan's antiwar songs served as anthems for the peace-loving counterculture.

The Beatles were instrumental in the counterculture music scene in large part due to the songs written by John Lennon and Paul McCartney, two of the Fab Four. Like Bob Dylan and Simon & Garfunkel, Lennon and McCartney both longed for peace and freedom, expressing this dream through their music. Lennon's most famous and most pointed plea for peace actually came about during his solo career in the early 1970s, with his song "Imagine," saying:

Imagine there's no countries
It isn't hard to do
Nothing to kill or die for
And no religion too
Imagine all the people
Living life in peace ...

You may say I'm a dreamer
But I'm not the only one
I hope someday you'll join us
And the world will be as one

The sentiment in that 1971 song was nothing new—Lennon's songs in the 1960s had similar messages of peace and acceptance, as did McCartney's.

But there was something more that vaulted the Fab Four to iconic status. Their music was *different*. It started out in a style similar to 1950s rock, but it quickly evolved to include inspiration from other genres, including **psychedelic** and hard rock, Indian music, and even classical. Each album released by the Beatles was innovative and different. If you look at the collection of albums recorded by the quartet in the 1960s, you can clearly trace the evolution of sound from the early hits like "Love Me Do" (1963) to the later experimental hits like

The Beatles onstage in London, circa 1963.

"Come Together" (1969). Not only are the lyrics of "Come Together" incredibly obscure and difficult to understand, but the sound of the melody is experimental and vastly different from early Beatles music.

That evolution of sound and style is a large part of what made the Beatles iconic. They started as four lads from Liverpool who appealed to American audiences when they crossed the pond and appeared on *The Ed Sullivan Show*. By the end of the decade, they were seen as deep, independent thinkers who challenged the system and weren't afraid to experiment with their music.

The Beatles broke up in 1970, but all four members experienced varying levels of success on their own. Paul McCartney and John Lennon could both be considered iconic as solo artists as well. Lennon's life was cut tragically short when he was shot at the age of forty by a former Beatles fan who reportedly was infuriated that Lennon had blasphemously described the Beatles as "more popular than Jesus."

AN EPIC FESTIVAL

Nowadays, music festivals aren't uncommon. But in the late 1960s, the Woodstock Festival was epic in proportion. The three-day festival drew half a million members of the counterculture from all over to a dairy farm in the small community of White Lake, New York, some 43 miles (69 kilometers) south of Woodstock, New York.

Thirty-two artists performed at the festival, which *Rolling Stone* magazine called one of the fifty moments that changed rock and roll history. Not all of the artists went on to major acclaim, but there were several iconic artists on the bill that weekend. Among the counterculture favorites were the Grateful Dead, Joan Baez, Janis Joplin, and Jimi Hendrix.

Like Bob Dylan and Simon & Garfunkel, Joan Baez was a folk singer-songwriter whose songs addressed antiwar sentiments, social justice, and civil and human rights. Still performing fifty years after her debut, Baez is known as much for her political and social activism as for her music. She has been heavily involved in causes ranging from civil rights to war protests to **LGBT** rights and poverty.

Another British Invasion

The Fab Four weren't the only Brits to storm the US music charts. In 1964, American counterculture got another dose of British rock in the form of the Rolling Stones, a London-based band formed in 1962. While the Beatles' music was inspired by many genres, the Rolling Stones' brand of rock and roll was largely based on the blues. They did stray into psychedelic rock for one album in the late 1960s, but most of their albums have been blues-infused rock.

The band's lineup has changed a bit over the years, but two constants are singer Mick Jagger and guitarist Keith Richards. Both men are iconic in their own right. Jagger is a ladies' man known for his sex appeal and dancing (even inspiring the 2010 Maroon 5 hit "Moves Like Jagger"), and certainly his singing has mass appeal. Along with Richards, he has also penned many of the Stones' biggest hits. Jagger is the face of one of the world's most successful and enduring bands. As of 2016, the Stones actually hold the record for the second-highest-grossing tour of all time, the Bigger Bang Tour of 2005–2007.

Keith Richards, on the other hand, has become an icon largely because he's still alive! Richards was born in 1943 and so isn't particularly old, but he is famous for his hard living and heavy drug use. His appearance shows the toll his years of hard living have taken, and there are even jokes with a punch line of "… but Keith Richards is still alive!" In 2010, BBC News actually published an article entitled "Who, What, Why: How Is Keith Richards Still Alive?" The answer to that question, according to addiction expert Dr. Rober Lefever, is that "he must have the constitution of an ox." All jokes aside, Richards claims he is actually *not* as hard living as the public thinks, and his real passion is not drugs, but books and libraries.

Janis Joplin, sometimes called the Queen of Psychedelic Soul, was the popular singer of "Piece of My Heart" (1968) and "Me and Bobby McGee" (1971), among other songs. Joplin's star burned fast and furious, though—she died at the age of twenty-seven, just three years after she and her band broke into the mainstream following their gig at the 1967 Monterey Pop Festival. Joplin had been a recovering drug user and alcoholic who relapsed when she found fame. Like so many icons, her untimely death only increased her popularity.

Some of Joplin's party pals were the members of the Grateful Dead, another iconic Woodstock band. Joplin and the Dead were both part of the San Francisco counterculture scene in the Haight-Ashbury neighborhood, and they regularly partied together. *Rolling Stone* magazine ranked the Dead as the fifty-seventh greatest artist of all time, and indeed they had a hugely powerful fan base of "Deadheads" who followed them around the country as they toured.

The Dead, whose best-known member was guitarist Jerry Garcia, had a unique style that included inspiration from numerous genres, including bluegrass, rock, psychedelic, and folk music. They were considered the ultimate jam band, favoring lengthy instrumental songs during their live performances.

The Dead had a long career, lasting from their formation in 1965 until Jerry Garcia's death following a heart attack while in rehab in 1995.

The ultimate icon of Woodstock, though, may have been the man who closed out the festival: Jimi Hendrix. Like more than a few rock stars of the era, Hendrix lived fast and died young—he died at twenty-seven, after only four years of fame. But what a four years it was! Jimi Hendrix is considered a master of the electric guitar—according to the

Legendary guitarist Jimi Hendrix was known for his performance stunts, which included playing the guitar behind his back and plucking the strings with his teeth.

Rock and Roll Hall of Fame, "the greatest instrumentalist in the history of rock music." His blues-infused style of rock was further defined by his masterful use of effects, such as gain, distortion, feedback, and wah—effects that are still used by rock guitarists today, more than forty years later. His feedback-driven version of "The Star-Spangled Banner" (1969) was an iconic performance that has gained millions of hits on YouTube. Ironically, the live performance was not seen by *that* many people at Woodstock; due to weather and other delays, Hendrix ended up performing on Monday morning, after most people had already left the festival.

Like many, Hendrix was iconic because of his masterful talent, but he became a true icon when he died so early in his career. There is a sense of *what if* that happens when a talented person dies long before the true extent of his or her talent is known. Such was the case with Hendrix, Joplin, and many others over the years.

GONE TOO SOON

As already mentioned, the 1960s brought the tragic death of President John F. Kennedy. It also claimed the life of the iconic blonde bombshell Marilyn Monroe when she died at age thirty-six. The 1960s also claimed the life of another iconic bombshell from the 1950s: actress, model, and singer Jayne Mansfield, who in fact was sometimes referred to as the "working man's [Marilyn] Monroe" and who was killed in a car accident at the age of thirty-four.

The 1960s also saw the premature deaths of two iconic members of the African-American community: Martin Luther King Jr. and Malcolm X. King was just thirty-nine years old when he was assassinated on the balcony of his hotel in Memphis, Tennessee, ending a life spent fighting for civil rights. A gifted orator, King is perhaps best known for his "I Have a Dream" speech, one of the most famous in United States history, and his "Letter from a Birmingham Jail" is considered a rhetorical masterpiece. King won the Nobel Peace Prize in 1964. His contributions to the civil rights movement were immeasurable; the motel where he was assassinated was later turned into the National Civil Rights Museum.

No less important in the African-American community was Malcolm X, although his work was markedly different from King's. While King preached peaceful, nonviolent

Two iconic leaders of the civil rights movement—Martin Luther King Jr. (*left*) and Malcolm X (*right*).

civil disobedience and was hugely influential in the civil rights movement, Malcolm X did not agree with King's stance on integration. Instead, he believed in the separation of black and white people. In fact, Malcolm X, as a member of the Nation of Islam, believed in black supremacy. He also disagreed with nonviolent disobedience and felt that African Americans should use any means to defend themselves and advance their position.

Both King and Malcolm X wanted to better the lives of black people in America, and they were both iconic among their supporters. They simply had two very different approaches to the same end goal.

DECADE IN REVIEW

The 1960s was a decade in turmoil. On the one hand, there was war and communism and the threat of nuclear attack and disillusionment with the government. On the other hand, there was the glittering ideal of Camelot during the Kennedy years and the peace and love–preaching hippies and the rising counterculture that demanded peace. All that turmoil made for a decade rich with icons.

THREE

1970s:

Disco, Blockbusters, and the "Me Decade"

THE 1960S WAS A DECADE OF CHANGE AND divisions. War loomed, and between the Cuban missile crisis and the Vietnam Conflict, Americans were deeply divided over whether the US even belonged in the middle of the conflict in Vietnam. And so, a counterculture formed, partly as a response to pro-military Americans and partly as a response to American big business, capitalism, and the traditional authority structure. Members of the counterculture wanted peace, freedom to express themselves, and freedom to be different. They weren't interested in the stereotypical family structure of the 1950s. They wanted freedom to create, to explore, and to love and live as they wished. This created a sense of community among the counterculture, and a sense of working together for a greater good.

That counterculture moved into the 1970s, but its form shifted a bit. Antiwar sentiments continued to grow. The fight for civil rights continued but changed—**Black Nationalism** that was championed by Malcolm X began to grow, while the peaceful protest that Martin Luther King Jr. had preached began to fade. And feminism gained tremendous footing during the 1970s. The movement had certainly existed during the 1960s, with more women starting to reject the traditional ideas of marrying out of high school. As the 1970s rolled on, more and more women began to speak out and demand equality. The 1973 *Roe v. Wade* Supreme Court decision, in which women were granted the right to choose to have an abortion, was emblematic for women's rights and certainly uniting for feminists. The landmark decision proved to be dividing as well, with Americans falling into pro-life and pro-choice camps. This ethical debate continues today. (Interestingly, the woman seeking an abortion who later admitted to being the plaintiff in the *Roe v. Wade* case ended up abruptly changing from pro-choice to pro-life activism.)

And while the counterculture of the 1960s had fostered a sense of community, in the 1970s it shifted to what author Tom Wolfe called the "me decade," in which people engaged in "the luxury … of dwelling upon the self." Americans, Wolfe thought, were now focused on recovering and being true to themselves—sometimes with little regard to the community around them.

THE "ME DECADE" AND THE PURSUIT OF PLEASURE

As part of the "me decade" and the associated voyage of self-discovery, people in the 1970s looked for new ways to find pleasure. For some, that meant experimenting with **hallucinogenic** drugs, which they thought brought them to a level of consciousness in which they could more fully explore their own psyche. For some, that meant participating in the sexual revolution that had begun in the 1960s—no longer did

Opposite: The counterculture was alive and well in the 1970s, with Vietnam War protestors spreading their message of peace.

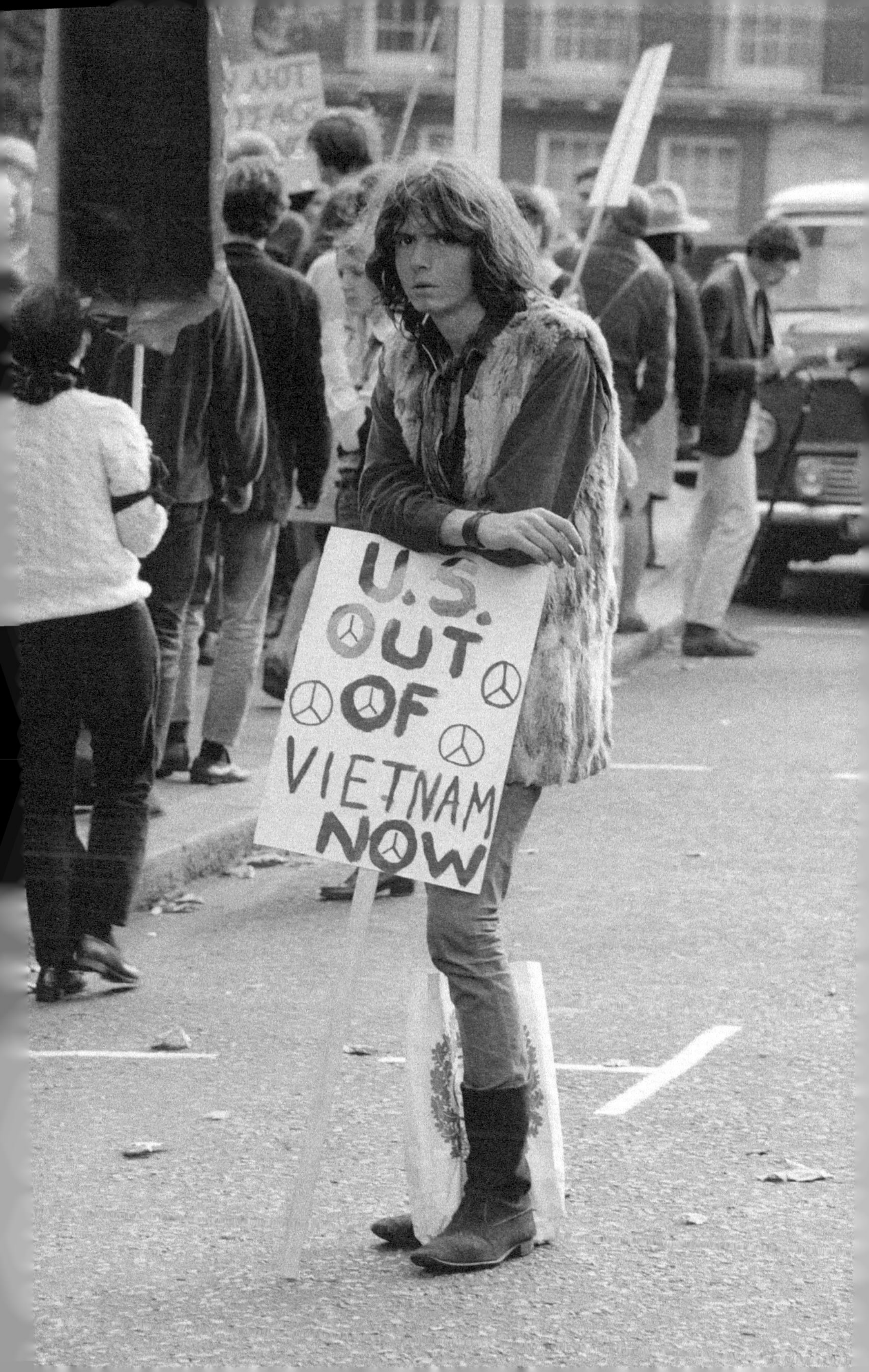
U.S.
OUT
OF
VIETNAM
NOW

all people save themselves for marriage and have their spouse be their one and only partner. People explored sexuality with partners before marriage.

But the sexual and drug revolutions had negative consequences. Venereal diseases spread—including AIDS, which was first recognized in 1981 but is believed to have spread widely during the sexual revolution of the 1970s. Additionally, drug experimentation carried plenty of risks—LSD was a widely used hallucinogen in the 1970s. Aside from the risk of overdose, it also carried the risk of long-term changes in perception or psychosis.

But there were harmless ways in which the "me generation" sought pleasure, too. One of them was dancing. The 1970s brought a new form of dance music known as disco. It was upbeat "club" music that integrated pop, soul, funk, and salsa. It was especially popular among women. Disco was also a bit of a response to the counterculture, which favored the heavy beats of rock music and found the disco beat and dance music to be frivolous.

In short, disco was *fun*. As such, it spawned a few iconic performers, including the Bee Gees and Donna Summer, as well as an iconic movie star: the young John Travolta.

THE QUEEN OF DISCO

If there ever was a Queen of Disco, it would have to be Donna Summer. In the 1960s, she had been a member of the counterculture and part of a psychedelic band. After spending time in Europe, she returned to the United States and relaunched her career as a disco artist. Her breakout hit, "Love to Love You Baby," released in late 1975, was actually banned by some radio stations for being a bit suggestive, but that didn't stop it from reaching **platinum** status. Summer followed up the success with numerous other hits and began to collect awards, including a total of five Grammys. By the late 1970s, Summer had become the first female artist to chart three number-one singles in one calendar year—an impressive feat for a woman whose music career started when she sang at church when she was eight years old.

THE THREE KINGS OF DISCO

If Donna Summer was the Queen of Disco, then the Bee Gees were certainly the three kings. The Gibb brothers—Barry, Robin, and Maurice—formed the Bee Gees in 1958, originally as a pop group. However, they became iconic not for their pop music but for their success on the disco scene. Their names might not be as familiar as, say, Elvis Presley or Michael Jackson, but the Bee Gees were phenomenally successful. In

The Gibb brothers, known as the Bee Gees, were kings in the disco world.

fact, they have been outsold by only five other artists: Presley, Jackson, the Beatles, Paul McCartney, and Garth Brooks. The Bee Gees' best-selling album, *Saturday Night Fever* (1977), was actually the highest selling album of all time until Michael Jackson's *Thriller* in the 1980s. The Rock and Roll Hall of Fame Museum describes the trio as "pioneers of dance-oriented pop."

So what made the Bee Gees iconic? For one thing, they were distinctive. Barry Gibb could reach a **falsetto** pitch that few male performers could hit. This sound became a trademark for the band. If you hear falsetto on a disco track, you can bet it is a Bee Gees song.

But the second piece of the puzzle was a little film called *Saturday Night Fever*. The Bee Gees recorded the soundtrack for the film. Both the movie and record became smash hits, thrusting disco into the mainstream—right as its appeal was starting to fade. Thanks to the record and film, disco was infused with new energy—and the Bee Gees rocketed to superstardom.

DISCO FEVER

The Bee Gees weren't the only ones who shot to stardom thanks to *Saturday Night Fever*. John Travolta, an up-and-coming young actor who'd had roles in a few television shows, movies, and live theater, became an overnight sensation when he landed the starring role of Tony Manero. Travolta played a working-class young man who finds local stardom as a dancer at a disco. The soundtrack was infectious, and the dancing was like nothing many Americans had ever seen—and it was a hit.

Opposite: John Travolta rocketed to superstardom after his turn as Tony Manero in *Saturday Night Fever*.

...where do you go when the record is over...
SATURDAY NIGHT FEVER

Travolta quickly followed up his success with *Grease* (1978), in which he starred as Danny Zuko, a bad boy who strives to win the heart of the wholesome Sandy Dumbrowski. Like *Saturday Night Fever*, the soundtrack to *Grease* was catchy and quickly became popular—although it was decidedly not disco. Rather, it was a retro nod to the 1950s, when the movie was set. And like Tony Manero in *Saturday Night Fever*, Danny Zuko could dance. So once again, Travolta danced into the hearts of the American public … and right into his status as an icon.

THE DAWN OF BLOCKBUSTER FILMS

Movies have been popular for decades—even before there was sound in films, the silent films drew crowds. But it wasn't until the 1970s that blockbuster movies became part of American culture.

A blockbuster film is simply a very, very successful film. The term is thought to have been first used in this context to refer to Steven Spielberg's *Jaws* (1975). Ever since, Spielberg has been the mastermind behind multiple blockbusters, including *Close Encounters of the Third Kind* (1977), *Raiders of the Lost Ark* (1981) (and its sequels), *E.T. the Extra-Terrestrial* (1982), *Back to the Future* (1985) (and its sequels), *Jurassic Park* (1993) (and many of its sequels), *Men in Black* (1997) (and its sequels), and *Transformers* (2007) (and its sequels).

In writing, directing, and/or producing these iconic film franchises, Spielberg himself has become an icon. If Steven Spielberg is attached to a film, it is almost guaranteed to be a mega-hit. He is thought to be one of the most influential moviemakers of all time, and in 2014, *Forbes* named him the most influential celebrity in the United States.

The interesting thing about Spielberg is that most American icons are always in the spotlight, and Spielberg is not. Because he spends his time behind the camera, he is not nearly as visible as the stars of iconic films.

Take, for example, the iconic stars of one of the most successful film franchises of all time: Star Wars. The original Star Wars film debuted in 1977 and was wildly popular. Its three stars—Harrison Ford as Han Solo, Carrie Fisher as Princess Leia, and Mark Hamill as Luke Skywalker—were immediately vaulted to superstar status. In the forty years

Mark Hamill and Carrie Fisher starred as Luke Skywalker and Princess Leia in the original Star Wars trilogy.

Icons in Children's Television

By the 1970s, televisions were in nearly every home, and TV stations discovered a previously untapped audience: children. *Mister Rogers' Neighborhood*, starring Fred Rogers as a kindly man who used puppets, characters, and music to teach children about different issues and concepts, had been on television in various forms for some years. It wasn't until the late 1960s that the show gained a wider audience. Following up on the success of *Mister Rogers' Neighborhood, Sesame Street* premiered in late 1969 and quickly gained a large viewership. While *Mister Rogers' Neighborhood* tended to teach life lessons and concepts, *Sesame Street* had a more academic focus, teaching letters and numbers to preschoolers. It was wildly appealing to its young audience, in large part because it used Jim Henson's Muppets as main characters. Big Bird, Cookie Monster, Oscar the Grouch, and later Elmo were icons in the eyes of the children who watched the show—and their creator, Jim Henson, was seen by parents as a bit of a genius.

Building on the success of *Sesame Street*, PBS broadcast *The Electric Company*, a children's television program designed to help children with grammar and reading skills. The show used humor that appealed to slightly older kids than the *Sesame Street* crowd. The original cast included actor Morgan Freeman and comedian Bill Cosby (who has since fallen into disgrace but at one time was an iconic performer).

Although children's television may not sound like the stuff of icons, if you asked any preschool child in the 1970s who the most famous person was, it's very likely that his or her answers would include some combination of Big Bird, Cookie Monster, and Mister Rogers. Icon status is sometimes in the eye of the beholder!

The 1969 cast of *Sesame Street*, including Muppets Big Bird, Oscar the Grouch, Bert, Ernie, Grover, and Cookie Monster.

since the first film was released, these stars are *still* identified as their characters, despite amassing a long list of acting credits beyond Star Wars. Carrie Fisher is still best known as Princess Leia. And Harrison Ford will forever be the handsome, swashbuckling Han Solo, despite also starring in the phenomenally successful Indiana Jones films and numerous other commercially and critically successful films.

What made these characters iconic? Well, without a good script and a good movie, they never would've gone anywhere. Moviegoers enjoyed the story behind Star Wars, and the special effects were groundbreaking for the time. But they also liked the trio of characters who led the movie. Princess Leia was the beautiful, strong, feminist princess, who was still soft enough to be wooed by Han Solo's roguish charm. Luke Skywalker was the good boy and talented Jedi determined to save the galaxy. And Han Solo was the brooding bad boy with the mad piloting skills who managed to swoop in and save the day whenever needed. His sarcastic wit and bad reputation made him the James Dean "rebel without a cause" of the series, and just as it had twenty years before with the real James Dean, that character sucked in moviegoers.

GONE TOO SOON

The 1970s wasn't necessarily a good decade to be an iconic musician. The world lost a number of major talents in the industry. Janis Joplin and Jimi Hendrix died just weeks apart, both at the age of twenty-seven. The following year, the lead singer for the Doors, Jim Morrison, also died at the age of twenty-seven. Elvis Presley passed away later in the decade, in 1977. The same story held true for Sid Vicious, the famed singer for the British punk band the Sex Pistols—and notorious for having possibly killed his girlfriend in a drug-induced haze.

Mama Cass Elliot, singer for the Mamas & the Papas, who earned fame in the 1960s with hits such as "Monday Monday" (1966) and "California Dreamin'" (1966), died from a heart attack at age thirty-two. (A story has long circulated that the overweight singer choked to death on a ham sandwich, but that is merely an urban legend. An autopsy showed the cause of death to be a heart attack.) American folk and rock singer Jim Croce died at the age of thirty in a plane crash, after gaining success with songs such as "Time in a Bottle" (1972) and "Bad, Bad Leroy Brown" (1973). And in 1977, a plane crash claimed the lives of four musicians from southern rock band Lynyrd Skynyrd, famed for their signature song "Sweet Home Alabama" (1974).

DECADE IN REVIEW

The 1970s were a decade of change and a decade of tragedy. People found a new resilience as they looked inside themselves as part of the "me decade," and women gained more and more freedom as feminist ideals gained traction. But wild lifestyles destroyed the lives of numerous icons, robbing the world of their future talent.

MTV landed on the television scene in the 1980s.

FOUR

1980s: The Pop Era

AFTER THE "ME DECADE" OF THE 1970S, American culture underwent another shift. After decades of living under the looming cloud of the **Cold War**, tensions began to ease. President Ronald Reagan and Mikhail Gorbachev, leader of the Soviet Union, came together to end the longstanding strain between the two nations by negotiating an end to the arms race. Under Gorbachev's leadership, the Soviet Union slowly emerged from under communist rule and ultimately disbanded. The Berlin Wall, which had divided the German city into the communist East and non-communist West, was opened in November 1989. On December 3, the Cold War was officially declared over.

However, while the Cold War was ending, a new threat was slowly emerging: terrorism. Tensions in the Middle East were growing, with wars and terrorist acts occurring. It is believed that al-Qaeda was started in the 1980s, with the rise of **Islamism.** Just as one threat was ending, another was emerging.

On the home front, a new threat appeared: a disease known as AIDS. It was first thought to be a disease strictly afflicting homosexual males. However, as more cases emerged and further research was done, people learned that AIDS was not restricted to the homosexual community. Eventually, it was determined that AIDS was a condition that could affect anyone and was transmitted by the exchange of bodily fluids—through unprotected intercourse, intravenous drug use, or even blood transfusions. America lived in a panic as they learned of Ryan White, who was diagnosed with HIV (the virus that causes AIDS) at age thirteen, resulting from a blood transfusion. That panic increased when the public learned of Kimberly Ann Bergalis, a young woman who contracted HIV/AIDS from her dentist, who was HIV positive.

Today, safeguards are in place to protect people from contracting HIV/AIDS, as long as they take precautions when engaging in sexual intercourse. But in the 1980s, when AIDS was newly discovered and details about its transmission were still emerging, it held the country in a panic.

But the 1980s wasn't only a decade of fear. Big, exciting changes were happening, too. Computer technology was growing rapidly, and the earliest forms of the Internet were beginning to show up in academia. The technology was still too new to be in people's homes, but it was becoming more widely used on college campuses and in the business world. It wouldn't be long before this new technology was everywhere.

VIDEO KILLED THE RADIO STAR

Before the Internet was commonplace, people had to find their entertainment in other places. Years ago, they found it in books. Then they turned to radio; families would gather around to listen to their favorite radio shows and broadcasts. Then came the television—a family favorite in the 1950s and 1960s. By the 1980s, television brought a new form of entertainment that combined the best in radio with the best in television: a little network called MTV.

MTV stood for Music Television, which is exactly what it was: a network that played music videos. While radio had music played by DJs, or disc jockeys, television now had MTV, with music videos played by VJs, or video jockeys.

Music on television wasn't in itself a new concept; millions of viewers had tuned in to programs like *The Ed Sullivan Show* for performances by Elvis Presley, the Beatles, and other famous artists. And shows like *American Bandstand* and *Soul Train* featured music and dancing. But MTV was a bit different. It didn't show everyday people dancing to popular music. Instead, it showed inventive, artful, creative videos of the performers themselves—virtually all day, every day. In its early days, MTV was mostly just music videos—it barely resembled the network it is today, with reality shows and other programming.

Amusingly, the first video chosen to be shown on the fledgling network, on August 1, 1981, was "Video Killed the Radio Star" by the Buggles—a song that questioned how technology would affect the arts.

MTV's popularity was immediate, and it didn't take long at all for it to affect music sales—suddenly, viewers were introduced to musicians they had never heard on the radio, and they liked it. The launch of MTV, in fact, is said to have sparked a second "British Invasion," where American audiences were introduced to British music acts that weren't played on the radio but that became wildly popular.

Not surprisingly, MTV helped launch some musical icons; two of the biggest were Madonna and Michael Jackson, who went on to become legendary performers.

THE BIGGEST JACKSON

Michael Jackson gained early fame as a member of the Jackson 5 in the 1960s and then as a solo artist in the 1970s. But he became an icon in the 1980s when he released his 1982 album *Thriller*. The album is still widely regarded as one of the most groundbreaking records in music history—and certainly the most profitable, given that it holds the record as the best-selling album of all time. Three hit songs from the album— "Billie Jean," "Beat It," and "Thriller"—had music videos that became phenomenally successful. "Thriller," in particular, was groundbreaking. The extended music video, which was fourteen minutes long, was a creepy, Halloween-themed masterpiece inspired by early horror films, complete with dancing zombies. It is still a cult favorite, but it achieved critical fame, too; in 2009, it became the first music video added to the National Film Registry.

But Michael Jackson's video success was not without a fight. Prior to releasing the video for "Billie Jean," MTV played very few videos by non-white artists, citing demographics and the fact that their audience preferred rock music, which wasn't traditionally performed by black artists. "Billie Jean," however, was such a popular song on the music charts that MTV eventually began to play it. Following the video's success, the network started to play other videos by Michael Jackson and eventually videos by other black artists.

None of Jackson's future albums ever matched the success of 1982's *Thriller*, but that's not to say they were unsuccessful. Jackson's follow-up album, 1987's *Bad*, was the first album to chart five number-one singles on the Billboard charts. His 1991

***Opposite*: During his 1980s reign as "The King of Pop," Jackson was often photographed sporting a military-style jacket, covered in sequins.**

(*Dangerous*) and 1995 (*HIStory*) albums also sold extremely well, though again, not as well as *Thriller*.

In later years, Jackson became known for his eccentricities as much as his talent. For a while, he famously lived with a chimp named Bubbles. There was a short-lived marriage to Elvis Presley's daughter, Lisa Marie, and a somewhat unusual desire to remain childlike, even turning his home into a sort of theme park called Neverland, the magical land of Peter Pan, the boy who never grows up.

Despite all of his eccentricities, Michael Jackson remained an icon. When he died in 2009, the world mourned. He is remembered as an iconic performer whose music touched millions.

THE 1980S QUEEN OF POP

Another mainstay on MTV in the 1980s was Madonna. She was already well known in the club scene for her songs "Everybody" and "Burning Up" when her third single, "Holiday," hit the charts in 1983. But it was her performance on MTV's Video Music Awards (VMAs) that launched her as an icon. Promoting her second album, *Like a Virgin*, Madonna chose to perform the title track at the 1984 VMAs, wearing a punkish wedding dress and white gloves in what was inimitable Madonna style.

Always one to push boundaries, Madonna played up her highly sexualized image, further scandalizing conservative parents, who wanted the song banned based on moral issues.

In the mid-1980s, Madonna ventured into film and ended up marrying Hollywood actor Sean Penn, a union that lasted

***Opposite*: Madonna performing at the 1984 MTV Video Music Awards.**

BOY TOY

four years. But lest the public think she had ventured too far into conventional territory, Madonna kept them on their toes by releasing the video for "Like a Prayer" (1989), which caused an uproar among Catholics for its use of Catholic symbols and themes of loose morals. So strong was the backlash that Pepsi canceled Madonna's endorsement deal with them. But ultimately the controversial video didn't hurt Madonna, who ended up being named Artist of the Decade for the 1980s by MTV and *Billboard* and *Musician* magazines.

Madonna kicked off the 1990s with a world tour that featured suggestive choreography, further angering her critics. In the early 1990s, Madonna's video for "Justify My Love" (1993) was banned by MTV for being too sexually explicit.

Midway through the 1990s, though, Madonna decided to tone down her image. Whether it was becoming a mother (to daughter Lourdes) or a response to the critical and public backlash that her sexual persona had gone too far, Madonna took it down a notch and began to be a bit more subdued. Emphasis on "a bit"—Madonna has never been one to back *too* far down from controversy.

Madonna continued to push boundaries in the late 1990s and early 2000s, and even now, in her fifties, Madonna is still regarded as an inventive and electric performer. She no longer inspires as much controversy as she did—leaving that job to younger performers such as Miley Cyrus now. Her music continues to show an ever-evolving style, and her long-term success as a musical artist is virtually unmatched.

KINGS AND QUEENS OF COMEDY

The 1980s was also a decade of funny men and women. Comedy was king at the box office and on television, and a whole herd of comedians rose to fame during the decade.

FROM *MORK* TO *MRS. DOUBTFIRE*

Among all of the talented comedians of the 1980s, one stands out as a true comic genius and an American icon: Robin Williams. Williams actually began his rise to fame in the 1970s, on the standup comedy scene. He became a household name in the late 1970s and early 1980s when he portrayed a lovable alien named Mork on TV's *Mork & Mindy*. Mork was originally a character on another popular show, *Happy Days*, but the guest appearance was so popular with audiences that Mork was given his own show.

Williams was a genius at improvisation, and part of the appeal to his comedy was that it was rarely scripted. Producers knew that Robin Williams would take a role and reinvent it with wild, off-the-cuff improvisation—which audiences loved. He was also a master of impersonations and could jump seamlessly from impression to impression at an almost manic pace.

Williams also did a number of comedy specials, but his popularity grew exponentially when he made the leap to the big screen. He starred in 1987's *Good Morning, Vietnam*, in which he portrayed a radio DJ who attempts to lift the spirits of troops in Vietnam with comedy. Williams gained wide critical and popular acclaim for the movie and was ultimately nominated for an Academy Award for his performance, though he didn't win.

That wasn't Williams's only shot at the prestigious award, though. He was also nominated for the dramatic films *Dead Poets Society* (1989) and *The Fisher King* (1991), and he won an Academy Award for Best Supporting Actor in the drama *Good Will Hunting* (1997).

Despite his comic genius, Williams actually acted in a surprising number of dramatic films, and children's films as well. One of his most popular roles was as the genie in the animated film *Aladdin* (1992). And of course, it would be impossible to forget Williams's much-loved turn as Daniel Hillard, the sentimental father who reinvents himself as Mrs. Doubtfire, a strict but loving housekeeper who is hired to take care of Daniel's children after his wife asks for a divorce.

Sadly, like many icons, Robin Williams was not destined for a long life. In 2014, he committed suicide at the age of sixty-three. Although rumors quickly spread that the suicide was due to a drug relapse and/or depression, the public later learned that Williams had been suffering from Parkinson's disease and Lewy body dementia, which would have likely claimed his life by natural causes within the next several years.

LIVE FROM NEW YORK!

Robin Williams was far from the only funny man of the 1980s. Comedies were wildly popular at the box office, and sitcoms were on all of the major television networks. One particular show took a slightly different approach, though. *Saturday Night Live* (*SNL*), which began its run in 1975, used the format of a variety show to showcase sketch comedy. Late on Saturday nights, viewers would tune into NBC to hear the familiar words: "Live from New York, it's Saturday night!" And so would begin ninety minutes of comedy sketches interspersed with musical performances.

SNL is notable for having introduced the public to several iconic comedians, including Eddie Murphy, John Belushi, Dan Aykroyd, Chevy Chase, Chris Farley, Gilda Radner,

Opposite: **Robin Williams, circa 1999.**

Bill Murray, Billy Crystal, Mike Myers, Dana Carvey, Adam Sandler, Tracy Morgan, Tina Fey, and Amy Poehler.

Because *SNL* has featured more than 140 comedians over its run, many of whom have gone on to find success, it's hard to choose a single standout. But certainly 1980s *SNL* produced an impressive number of comedians who went on to find success on the big screen. Eddie Murphy, for example, wasn't on *SNL* for very long, but it was long enough for him to make a name for himself and land roles in such popular movies as *Coming to America* (1988) and the Beverly Hills Cop series. Murphy later found success as the voice of Donkey in the Shrek films—which were the brainchild of another 1980s and 1990s *SNL* veteran, Mike Myers (also famed for the Austin Powers movies).

One of Mike Myers's most popular *SNL* characters was Wayne Campbell in the "Wayne's World" sketches. Myers's partner in those sketches was Dana Carvey—one of the big names from *SNL* in the 1980s. Carvey played rocker-wannabe Garth Algar in the sketches. But Carvey could not be typecast as simply the dropout rocker—during his years on *SNL*, he was also famed for his impersonations of President George H. W. Bush and presidential candidate Ross Perot.

GONE TOO SOON

In addition to the *SNL* cast members who died young, the 1980s saw a number of other deaths of iconic stars. Bob Marley, the highly acclaimed and very popular reggae artist, died of malignant melanoma in 1981, at the age of thirty-six.

***Opposite*: The 1986 cast of *Saturday Night Live*.**

SATURDAY
NIGHT
LIVE

Marley's doctor had urged him to have his toe amputated when the cancer was discovered, but Marley, a devout **Rastafarian**, refused, saying it conflicted with his religious beliefs. The cancer later spread throughout his body, leading to his death.

Marley was far from the only musician to die prematurely in the 1980s. The iconic John Lennon was assassinated by a crazed former fan in 1980. Motown and soul artist Marvin Gaye was shot at the age of forty-four by his father, reportedly because Gaye intervened in a dispute between his parents. Andy Gibb, a successful solo artist and brother of the iconic disco band the Bee Gees, died at the age of thirty of heart inflammation. Bon Scott, lead singer of the iconic rock band AC/DC, died in 1980 of alcohol poisoning, at the age of thirty-three. And John Bonham, drummer for the iconic British rock band Led Zeppelin, died at the age of thirty-two after choking to death on his own vomit.

Another singer who died prematurely in the 1980s was an icon on the rise: Karen Carpenter, who sang along with her brother as part of the duo the Carpenters, died at age thirty-two of heart failure caused by anorexia. Carpenter may have died before she had a chance to become a legend, but her death certainly brought awareness to the very real problem of anorexia, which had not been covered in the media much before her death.

DECADE IN REVIEW

The 1980s was an interesting mix of reconciliation (the end of the Cold War), turmoil (the rising conflict in the Middle East), and fear (the AIDS crisis). But amid it all, America found icons in music and in comedy.

The *Saturday Night Live* Curse

With a cast numbering somewhere above 140 members over its forty years on the air, it's not entirely surprising that *Saturday Night Live* would have a few cast members who didn't live to old age. But unfortunately, *SNL* has had more than a few of its cast members die prematurely:

- John Belushi, an early *SNL* cast member, died of a drug overdose at age thirty-three.
- Gilda Radner, another early cast member who was groundbreaking as a successful comedian in a male-dominated field, died at age forty-two from ovarian cancer.
- Jan Hooks, another female cast member from the 1980s who was famous for her Hillary Clinton impersonations, died at age fifty-seven of cancer.
- Andy Kaufman, an early cast member, died of lung cancer at age thirty-five.
- Danitra Vance, *SNL*'s first black female cast member, died of breast cancer at age thirty-five.
- Chris Farley, a member of the 1990s cast who achieved considerable success on the big screen, died at age thirty-three of a drug overdose.
- Phil Hartman, another 1990s cast member, was shot to death at age forty-nine by his wife.

President George Bush Sr. visited American troops serving in the Gulf War during Thanksgiving in 1990.

FIVE

1990s: Politics and a New Media

THE CLOSE OF THE 1980S MIGHT HAVE brought the official end of the Cold War, but it certainly didn't bring the ever-elusive world peace. The war and subsequent dissolution of Yugoslavia into separate countries figured prominently in the world history of the early to mid-1990s. Several countries in Africa experienced political tensions, civil wars, and **genocide**, and while the United States wasn't actively involved in much of that, the media brought horrifying news of the deaths in Africa and in Europe.

But the Middle East was another story. Tensions were still high there, with al-Qaeda growing, the Taliban continuing to rise in power, and dictator Saddam Hussein presiding over Iraq. After Hussein ordered a successful invasion of Kuwait, the United States entered the conflict and sent troops into the Persian Gulf, kicking off the Gulf War. The Gulf War itself wasn't terribly long—just a few months in late 1990 and early 1991—but it kicked off a US military presence in the Middle East that lasted throughout the 1990s. Even the end of the Gulf War didn't do much to ease the tension with the Middle East.

In 1993, this continuing tension became evident in a terrorist attack on the World Trade Center. Several men with links to al-Qaeda planned and carried out a bombing of the World Trade Center that was designed to bring down both towers. The attack was largely unsuccessful yet still tragic—the bomb damaged the underground parking structure in which it was detonated and ultimately killed six people and injured more than a thousand others, but it did not bring down the towers as planned.

Reportedly, the motive for the bombing was to force the United States to end its interference in Middle Eastern affairs. The terrorists were upset at continued US support of Israel, with whom they were in conflict. Even if not ultimately successful, the attack certainly opened Americans' eyes to the fact that the United States was not very popular with some Middle Easterners.

But in 1995, Americans were reminded that not all terrorism comes from overseas. Caucasian, American-born Timothy McVeigh and Terry Nichols bombed a federal building in Oklahoma City, killing 168 people and injuring nearly 700 others, because of their dislike of the federal government. McVeigh had actually served in the Gulf War, but his motive for the bombing in Oklahoma City was reportedly his dislike of how the federal government had handled a couple of domestic incidents. These included the Waco siege, when the Bureau of Alcohol, Tobacco, Firearms and Explosives and the FBI raided a ranch held by a religious group known as the Branch Davidians, and the Ruby Ridge incident, where United States marshals and the FBI ultimately killed two members of a family who were believed to be members of the Aryan Nation and involved in various illegal weapons activities. Terry Nichols,

McVeigh's co-conspirator, was similarly distrustful of the government, despite having also served in the military.

Part of what made events like these so raw and real to the American public was the increasing spread of the media in the 1990s. Television and newspapers had been reporting on such incidents for years, of course, but with cable television widespread, most households had access to far more news sources than they had in the past. And the mid- to late 1990s brought an entirely new form of media: the Internet.

As commonplace as the World Wide Web is today, it's hard to imagine a world without the Internet. But just two decades ago, the Internet was in its infancy with the general public. The early technology had been around for some years, but it wasn't until the mid- to late 1990s that everyday people began to have access to it.

The Internet brought the World Wide Web and the chance to access news and information with just a few keystrokes and mouse clicks, but it also brought e-mail and instant messaging services, so people could share this information rapidly. Read a story about a domestic terror incident? You could e-mail it to everyone you knew in a matter of seconds!

And so, the world became intimately more connected—and people loved it. They enjoyed the immediate gratification of e-mail and instant messaging, and being able to look things up in seconds instead of going to the local library. It's safe to say that the Internet was the defining technological advancement of the 1990s, a decade where technological advancements were many.

A PRESIDENT AND A SCANDAL

Advancements in media meant that the president in the 1990s was under closer public scrutiny than any other president up to that point. And William Jefferson Clinton was certainly an interesting subject—at times wildly popular and at times controversial. The public had the means to hear *everything* about him, and they certainly took advantage of it.

Bill Clinton served as president for the majority of the decade—from 1993 to 2001. From the beginning, he was relatively popular (at least among the non-Democrat-hating crowd). He was relatively young (in his forties); was charismatic; had a smart, powerful wife; and had a young daughter. In some ways, he was very relatable. Even his campaign theme song in 1992 was relatable to the public—Fleetwood Mac's "Don't Stop" from their wildly successful 1970s rock album *Rumours*.

Clinton would've likely gone down in history as just another president—albeit a popular one—if it wasn't for a White House intern and a sex scandal. In 1998, during Clinton's second term in office, it became public knowledge that a White House intern less than half of the president's age had confessed to a coworker that she'd had an intimate relationship with the president during his first term in office. Monica Lewinsky, the intern in question, had originally denied the affair in a sworn affidavit, and Clinton denied the affair while under oath. However, Lewinsky eventually admitted to the affair and provided evidence that proved the president had lied about his involvement with her. Because Clinton had lied under oath, he was held in contempt of court, and the House of Representatives called for his **impeachment**. However, the Senate voted to acquit him, and Clinton ultimately retained the presidency despite his crime.

The Lewinsky scandal turned Clinton into an icon of sorts—certainly not a hero, but definitely a topic of discussion in nearly every home in America. Even those families who

Charismatic President Bill Clinton, circa 1995.

largely ignored politics were aware of the scandal, which was widely covered on every news network and discussed online.

THE FACE OF A NEW GENRE

The 1970s introduced America to the genre of disco, and the 1990s introduced America to another new genre that couldn't be much more different from the danceable tunes of the disco era. Grunge actually began in the 1980s, but it didn't become widely popular until the early 1990s—and when it did, its popularity spread quickly.

While disco was all about danceability, grunge was about the expression of frustration. The raw, hard beats weren't particularly danceable; they were more similar to heavy metal and punk.

Grunge began in Seattle, Washington, and put the Northwest city on the musical map. And the main face of Seattle's new grunge genre was a twenty-something by the name of Kurt Cobain. Cobain was the lead singer of Nirvana. He played such an iconic role in the grunge movement that after his death in 1994, *Time* magazine referred to him as

Kurt Cobain, the lead singer and guitarist of grunge band Nirvana, in 1991.

NOTORIOUS!

Not all icons are lily-white in terms of their background; certainly Bill Clinton had his secrets, and many of the musical and acting icons over the decades have had tumultuous personal lives. But some icons go beyond that—some are downright notorious. Those people enter into the consciousness of popular culture by virtue of the sheer *badness* of their misdeeds.

In the late 1960s, Charles Manson was the notorious leader of the Manson Family. He and his "family members" murdered nine people over five weeks in the summer of 1969. Playing off a Beatles song called "Helter Skelter," Manson hoped that the murders would set off a race war. He became a pop culture icon by virtue of his insanity and violence.

The late 1960s and early 1970s had another notorious icon: the Zodiac Killer. Like Manson, the Zodiac operated in California, but while Manson was in Southern California, the Zodiac's hunting ground was the San Francisco Bay Area. Authorities have pinned at least seven crimes in a ten-month span in the late 1960s on the Zodiac, though in his taunting letters to the authorities, the Zodiac claims to have killed at least thirty-seven people. The Zodiac has never been caught and his identity is unconfirmed; technically, it is still an open case.

California was the hunting ground for an iconic killer of the 1980s as well—a man named Richard Ramirez, whom the press dubbed the Night Stalker. The Night Stalker terrorized Los Angeles and the San Francisco Bay Area from mid-1984 to mid-1985, ultimately murdering at least fifteen people and savagely attacking many others.

The notorious face of the 1990s was less obviously vicious than Manson, the Zodiac, or the Night Stalker—it wasn't a serial killer terrorizing entire cities. Rather, it was that of a former football hero, O. J. Simpson. Simpson was arrested for the brutal murder of his ex-wife, Nicole Brown Simpson, and her friend, Ronald Goldman. He was later acquitted of the charges, but not before a very long and very public trial—and a notorious slow-speed chase in a white Ford Bronco that ended in Simpson's arrest.

the Northwest's John Lennon. Indeed, even with several rival grunge bands from Seattle, such as Pearl Jam and Alice in Chains, gaining widespread popularity, Nirvana stood out. Their second album, 1991's *Nevermind*, sold one million copies within its first nine weeks of release, spent almost five years on the *Billboard* charts, and had sold thirty million copies worldwide by 2011. Its first single, "Smells Like Teen Spirit," crossed over into mainstream popularity and vaulted the band—and its front man, Cobain—to stardom.

Cobain became iconic because he was the face of a band that launched a new genre into the music world. But, like so many icons, he became forever cemented as such because of his personal struggles and early death. Cobain struggled with heroin addiction and depression, and his marriage to fellow musician Courtney Love was tumultuous at best. The two had a young daughter, Frances Bean. Cobain was just twenty-seven when he committed suicide in his Seattle home.

THE DIVA ERA

Men weren't the only ones making music headlines in the 1990s. A number of female solo artists rose to fame, many of them classed as "divas." Technically, that term can be used to refer to any female pop singer, but generally the female musicians referred to as divas were rather temperamental and exacting in their expectations.

The divas of the 1990s included Celine Dion, a French-Canadian singer who has achieved worldwide fame for many songs and won five Grammys. Dion is probably best known for singing the theme song for the movie *Titanic*—"My Heart Will Go On" (1997). Songbird Mariah Carey's soaring vocals brought her fame with her 1990 debut album. She continued on to have numerous successful albums and an acting career. Britney Spears and Christina Aguilera, both former actresses on *The Mickey Mouse Club*, found fame as pop stars in the late 1990s.

But the ultimate iconic pop diva of the 1990s was Whitney Houston. Houston actually rose to fame in the 1980s, when her first album became the best-selling debut album ever by a woman. However, her fame grew exponentially in the 1990s, when she released more chart-topping songs and made the jump to acting with a starring role opposite Kevin Costner

Pop diva Whitney Houston sparkles onstage during a 1991 concert.

in 1992's *The Bodyguard*. The movie in itself was popular, but Houston's performance of the film's theme song, "I Will Always Love You," was wildly popular—ultimately becoming the best-selling single by a woman ever.

That song was actually written by another diva—Dolly Parton—who was primarily a highly successful country music singer but who has occasionally made the jump over to the pop charts. Parton's version of "I Will Always Love You" topped the country charts twice, but it was Houston's version that led to its mainstream popularity. Much like Celine Dion's "My Heart Will Go On," Houston's "I Will Always Love You" received so much airplay that some fans eventually got sick of it!

PAVING THE WAY FOR LGBT CELEBRITIES

In the mid-1990s, comedian Ellen DeGeneres launched her self-titled sitcom, *Ellen*, which was quite popular with American audiences. Quite popular, that is, until Ellen revealed in a 1997 interview with Oprah Winfrey that she was a lesbian. The revelation was written into the storyline of the show, too, and the show began to tackle the issues relevant to the LGBT community. It's impossible to say whether this is what caused the downfall of the show, as the 1997–1998 season of *Ellen* ended up being its last. Naturally, fans wondered. Were Americans not yet ready for an openly gay character on a major television show? Ellen's revelation of her sexuality, as well as the portrayal of an openly gay character on the show, resulted in awards but also brought frightened sponsors, lost viewers, and even bomb threats.

But at the same time, Ellen's move was groundbreaking. Slowly, it became more acceptable to audiences and sponsors to have a show with major characters who were homosexual. *ER*, another popular series from the 1990s and 2000s, featured several homosexual characters. Cable networks produced series

Ellen DeGeneres landed on the cover of *Time* magazine when she came out as a lesbian, but her show quickly fell out of favor and was soon canceled.

such as *Queer as Folk* and *The L Word*. Even teen-aimed shows, such as *The O.C.* and *Gossip Girl*, began to tackle LGBT issues. And one of the most popular series of the 2010s, *Modern Family*, features a homosexual couple in a lead role. In exposing her sexuality and addressing it head-on in her show, Ellen paved the way for LGBT celebrities who came after her.

But it wasn't an easy time for Ellen. In an interview with *20/20*, Ellen describes the time period surrounding her coming out, the resulting backlash, and her show's cancellation by saying, "It destroyed me. For somebody who makes a living trying to make people happy and trying to please everybody and wanting so desperately to be loved ... to all of a sudden feel like you're not only not loved—you're hated."

Ellen bounced back in the most unlikely of ways: as the voice of an endearing, forgetful blue fish named Dory. The writer of *Finding Nemo* (2003) wrote the part of Dory with DeGeneres in mind, and in 2016, the popular fish returned to the big screen in her own movie, *Finding Dory*. Also in 2003, Ellen cemented her return as an A-list celebrity when she launched her daytime talk show, *The Ellen DeGeneres Show*, which won four Daytime Emmy Awards in its first season alone.

Throughout her rise and fall and then her rise back to fame, Ellen has remained true to herself, with her signature kindness and humor. Audiences may have initially been intimidated by a lifestyle unknown to them, but Ellen is nothing if not persistent, cheerful, and willing to work hard. She didn't pursue her cause by getting angry; rather, she stayed unapologetic, true to her beliefs, and always entertaining. That combination of traits was likely a factor in drawing audiences back to her and opening the doors for others to follow.

GONE TOO SOON

Like every decade, the 1990s had its share of iconic personalities who died too soon. Perhaps the most notable among those was Diana, Princess of Wales. She was killed in a car accident at the age of thirty-six, after being pursued by **paparazzi** through the streets of Paris. Tragically, Diana left her two young sons, Princes William and Harry, motherless at a young age.

America has long had a fascination with the British royal family, but Diana was an icon because she was the "people's princess." The royal family had traditionally been seen as rather untouchable and unapproachable, but Diana was a shy kindergarten teacher who'd caught the eye of the prince, whom she had known most of her life. In a fairytale wedding watched on television by millions, Diana married Charles in 1981. This was the first big British royal wedding to be made public—Queen Elizabeth II, Charles's mother, had married in 1947, long before televisions were in homes and such events were broadcast to the public at large. From the start, Diana's royal life was different from that of previous royals. She was a hands-on mother to her sons who delighted in taking them out to public places instead of sheltering them in the royal palaces. She also involved them in her work with AIDS patients and in homeless shelters. Diana never stood back from those she was helping, simply bringing a royal face to an issue. For example, she was very hands-on with AIDS patients, which was unusual given that at the time the crisis was spreading and it wasn't entirely known how the disease was spread and how contact might affect people.

Diana and Charles ultimately divorced—quite unusual in the royal family—but she remained a highly public figure, both for her charitable works and for her inimitable style. When she died in 1997, the world mourned her loss.

The music world suffered the loss of several icons in the 1990s as well. In addition to Kurt Cobain, legendary electric guitarist Stevie Ray Vaughan was killed in a helicopter crash in 1990. Freddie Mercury, lead vocalist of the rock band Queen, died of AIDS in 1991 at the age of forty-five, just twenty-four hours after admitting to the press that he had the disease. In 1993, Selena Quintanilla-Pérez, a phenomenally successful Latin artist who was crossing over into the mainstream pop world, died at the age of twenty-three after being shot by a member of her staff who had been embezzling money from her. Tupac Shakur, legendary in the rap genre, was shot to death in 1996. Some questions exist as to whether rival rapper Notorious B.I.G. was involved in Tupac's death, but that question will likely never be answered. Biggie himself died in a drive-by shooting less than a year later—possibly due to involvement in Tupac's death, but that mystery, too, is unlikely to be solved.

DECADE IN REVIEW

The 1990s was an amazing decade of development in terms of the Internet, which brought all of the 1990s icons closer to the American people. It was a time of mounting tensions with the Middle East, but also a time of amazing developments in music and technology. The 1990s prepared the way for America to move into an entirely new millennium.

SIX

2000s: Reality and Magic

AMERICA ROLLED INTO THE 2000S ON A WAVE of fear. Many believed that Y2K, the common term for "the year 2000," referring to the moment when 1999 became 2000, would spell worldwide chaos. Why? Because technology was an integral part of the functioning world, and computers—the heart of technology—were not necessarily equipped to deal with a twenty-first-century date. Computers generally used the last two digits of the year—just as we say '99 when referring to the year 1999, so, too, would computers—and so there was widespread fear that when the date changed to the year 2000, computers would misinterpret the 00 as 1900, and technological chaos would ensue.

Luckily, the fears turned out to be relatively pointless—most corporations and entities were able to address the problem and upgrade their systems so that computers could recognize the year 2000. And so began not just a new decade, not just a new century, but an entirely new millennium.

Just as the 1990s had its share of political tensions, so, too, did the 2000s. The situation in the Middle East was still not resolved. In fact, on a sunny morning in

Y2K was a looming fear for many Americans as the 1990s drew to a close.

September 2001, it became clear that the situation was worse than ever. As Americans on the East Coast were arriving at work on the morning of September 11, and as Americans on the West Coast were just waking up for the day, American Airlines Flight 11 crashed into the north tower of the World Trade Center. At first it seemed to be a terrible accident, but just seventeen minutes later, United Airlines Flight 175 crashed into the south tower, and it became very clear that this was a coordinated terrorist attack. Half an hour later, American Airlines Flight 77 crashed into the Pentagon in Washington, DC, and another thirty minutes later, United Airlines Flight 93 crashed into a field near Shanksville, Pennsylvania, after passengers attempted to overpower the hijackers, who reportedly planned to crash the plane into the White House. Within two hours, both towers of the

World Trade Center had collapsed. In total, the events of September 11, 2001, claimed nearly three thousand lives.

The terror attacks, the deadliest in United States history, were organized by al-Qaeda and masterminded by its leader, Osama bin Laden. The United States responded to the attacks by initiating the War on Terror, which continued until President Barack Obama declared it over on May 23, 2013.

The War on Terror certainly dominated the American consciousness in the 2000s, but the 9/11 attacks weren't the only catastrophic event. In late August 2005, the deadly Hurricane Katrina struck the Gulf of Mexico and the Louisiana coast, claiming well over a thousand people's lives and yielding property damage of roughly $108 billion. Aside from the obvious devastation brought by the hurricane and the lives lost, the storm generated a great deal of controversy because many believed that government agencies and officials did not respond in an appropriate manner, which ended up causing even more devastation than the initial fallout from the storm.

And just three years later, in 2008, the United States experienced turmoil on the financial front as the country entered a deep recession and the crash of the real-estate market. For years, conventional wisdom had dictated that people bought homes and gained value in them as the years progressed. But suddenly, millions of Americans were left with mortgages they couldn't pay and homes that were worth only a fraction of what they had bought them for. The job market was in tatters, and people who had previously held high-powered jobs were fighting to get any sort of work they could find.

But there was hope that same year, in the form of a new president: Barack Obama, the first African American to be elected to the White House.

UNREAL REALITY

The turmoil of the 2000s left American audiences hungry for some sort of escape. For many, that escape came in the form of reality television.

Reality TV has actually been around in some form for decades. In the late 1940s, for example, the show *Candid Camera* showed pranks being pulled on real people while they were secretly recorded. And in the 1980s and 1990s, tabloid-style talk shows were popular. But reality TV as we now know it really came to the forefront in the 2000s, when shows such as *Survivor, American Idol, Dancing with the Stars,* and *The Bachelor* gained huge followings.

Plenty of Americans find reality TV distasteful and refuse to watch it, calling it "scripted" or "exploitative." But there are many more who eagerly tune in and suspend their disbelief as they watch to see which contestant will be voted off next or who will take home the top prize. And whether you like reality TV or not, it's impossible to not know the names of some of the most iconic people from it.

One of the major complaints about reality stars is that some of them become famous for no particular reason—they don't have any particular talent, but they're thrust upon the American public. Somehow, they end up with staying power. Such is the case with an entire family of icons from the 2000s: the Kardashians.

The name "Kardashian" was somewhat known back in the 1990s, when Robert Kardashian became a televised face as a member of O. J. Simpson's defense team in 1995. By that time, Kardashian was already divorced from his wife, Kris, the mother of his four children: Kourtney, Kim, Khloé, and Rob. Kris had quickly remarried Bruce Jenner, a former Olympian (now known as Caitlyn) and had two more children:

The Kardashians in 2016.

Kendall and Kylie. The family became widely known after the premiere of their reality television show, *Keeping Up with the Kardashians* (*KUWTK*), in 2007; however, daughter Kim was already somewhat well known as the friend of socialite Paris Hilton.

The Kardashians are a classic case of a family made popular for reasons no one can quite explain. When *KUWTK* premiered, the family wasn't particularly noteworthy. Kim was known from her friendship with Hilton, and Kris was somewhat known for being married to former Olympian Jenner, but that was about as far as it went. And yet, millions of Americans were fascinated by the family and tuned in to watch the show. The Kardashian family seemed to revel in the attention and turned their sudden fame into an incredibly lucrative empire. And the standout of the family is undoubtedly Kim, who has turned fame into a multimillion-dollar enterprise. Her fame only increased in 2014, when she married rap megastar Kanye West in a lavish $12 million wedding. As of 2016, Kim is reportedly worth somewhere in the neighborhood of $85 million.

A WORLD OF MAGIC

In a stark contrast to "famous for being famous" reality stars such as the Kardashians comes a famously private, formerly broke writer from the United Kingdom who just happened to write a book that inspired a love of reading in millions of children worldwide.

Joanne (J. K.) Rowling actually came up with the idea for Harry Potter in 1990 and published the first book in the United Kingdom in 1997. However, it wasn't until the 2000s that global Potter-mania really took hold. The first book in the seven-book series, *Harry Potter and the Sorcerer's Stone* (*Harry Potter and the Philosopher's Stone* in its UK publication), was published in the United States in 1998. By the time the fourth book, *Harry Potter and the Goblet of Fire,* was released in 2000, the series—and its author—were a full-fledged American obsession. Children who hadn't previously been particularly interested in reading dove into the incredibly long books, eager to see what each novel would bring for its main characters, Harry Potter, Ron Weasley, and Hermione Granger. The final book in the series, *Harry Potter and the Deathly Hallows,* is the fastest-selling book of all time, with a total of eleven million copies sold in the United States and United Kingdom on its first day of release.

Like any wildly popular pop culture phenomenon, the Harry Potter series was spun off into other lucrative ventures: movies, toys, and even theme parks. The Harry Potter brand is thought to be worth $15 billion, all told.

***Opposite*: British actor Daniel Radcliffe played young wizard Harry Potter in the films based on J. K. Rowling's best-selling novels.**

GRYFFINDOR

Meanwhile, the icon behind this mega-empire continues to live a quiet life in the United Kingdom, famously private and happiest when with her husband and children. Rowling is beyond rich—although she reportedly no longer qualifies as a billionaire because she has given much of her wealth away to charity and is subject to the high taxes in the United Kingdom. Today, she continues to write, and is also involved in numerous charities and philanthropic engagements.

A SWIFT ASCENT TO STARDOM

When the year 2000 rolled around, a little girl from Wyomissing, Pennsylvania, was just barely eleven years old. Yet just six years later, she released her first country album, *Taylor Swift*, and quickly made a name for herself as a rising country star.

But Swift didn't just make a splash in the country music scene. Songs from her debut album crossed over to the pop charts, and Swift quickly gained fame there as well. Her second album, *Fearless* (2008), was an immediate hit, earned Swift four Grammys, and ultimately became the best-selling album of 2009. Swift quickly followed up the success of *Fearless* with *Speak Now* (released in 2010) and *Red* (released in 2012), both also successes. And by the time she released *1989* in 2014, Swift was a full-fledged pop icon, and its first single released, "Shake It Off," became the anthem of the summer. The record-breaking *1989* album later earned Swift her second Grammy for album of the year.

What makes Swift different from many other "pop princesses" is that she is not just a singer, she is a songwriter.

***Opposite*: Taylor Swift at the Grammys in 2015.**

AWARDS

She dreamed of success at a young age, and by twelve she had decided that to make a name for herself, she needed to start writing her own material. When she was fourteen, Swift's family moved to the Nashville area in the hopes of encouraging her career, and she quickly landed a deal with RCA. Although she was young, songwriters and executives in Nashville recognized her raw talent.

Despite her amazing talent and success, Swift is not without her critics. She is known for writing songs based on her personal experiences—which means any and all of her ex-boyfriends are prime territory. Naturally, that has not sat well with some. She also famously feuded with pop star Katy Perry. Their spat reportedly inspired the hit single "Bad Blood" from Swift's *1989* album, although Swift declines to confirm whether that is true.

But despite people's concern about becoming material for her songwriting, Swift is generally well liked. She's known to be a "people person"—in fact, in 2012 she was compared to another icon when the *Hollywood Reporter* described her as "the Best People Person since Bill Clinton." And her contribution to pop culture can't be denied—Chuck Klosterman from GQ described Swift as "the most significant pop artist of the modern age." Significant indeed. And at not even thirty years old.

EQUALITY AND ACCEPTANCE FOR ALL

The 2000s also brought about a more mainstream acceptance of celebrities whose lifestyles would have been considered controversial in decades past. Although comedian and gay rights activist Ellen DeGeneres had come out in the late 1990s, her decision to share her homosexuality with America was not widely supported. Throughout the 2000s, sexual orientation has slowly lost the stigma it once held, and in 2015, the Supreme Court legalized same-sex marriage across the United States. That same year, former Olympian Bruce Jenner publicly announced that he was transgender. Jenner adopted the name Caitlyn and is living openly as a woman after years of struggling with gender identity. Jenner has received support from the Kardashians, who applaud her decision to live as a woman. Although Jenner is now living as a woman, she has not yet had gender-reassignment surgery and is unsure of whether she will. Certainly, Jenner's place in the public eye has opened doors for other transgender people as well. Actress Laverne Cox, who is transgender herself and portrays a transgender inmate on the Netflix series *Orange Is the New Black,* is also

Caitlyn Jenner at the 2016 Oscars.

THROWBACK ICONS

One of the most popular cable shows of the 2000s brought about an interesting twist: throwback icons. The show was *Mad Men*, and it began in 2007 and ran for seven seasons. *Mad Men* was set in the 1960s and early 1970s at a Madison Avenue advertising agency, and the series revolved around Don Draper, the creative director for the agency. Don was the quintessential 1960s ad man—well dressed, charming, creative, and willing to do whatever it took to reel in a client. His days at the office consisted of long, alcohol-fueled lunches with clients and colleagues and the occasional flash of brilliance that made him highly sought after in the industry. He was quiet, dark, and brooding, while being intensely charming—and the combination was irresistible to women. His wife, Betty, was a Grace Kelly–esque beauty who stayed home as a dissatisfied housewife. And his protégée, Peggy Olson, was the newly ambitious woman of the 1960s, not content to get married, stay home, and have children. The cast of *Mad Men* represented a bygone era, but American audiences were fascinated by these people, who for many bore a strong resemblance to their families growing up. And for some, the allure of the 1960s was fascinating—it was a patriarchal era strikingly different from anything they knew. In short, the iconic cast of *Mad Men* was retro-cool.

experiencing greater widespread acceptance now. Through icons such as DeGeneres, Jenner, and Cox, many people across the United States and around the world have found the courage and inspiration to be true to themselves.

GONE TOO SOON

The 2000s have brought their share of icons gone too soon. The loss of music legend Michael Jackson was felt far and wide. Although Jackson was seen as somewhat of an enigma, the impact he had on music and pop culture cannot be denied, and his relatively young death shocked the American public.

The death of actor Heath Ledger at age twenty-eight also sent shockwaves through the American public. Ledger starred in numerous successful films, and his portrayal of the Joker in *The Dark Knight* (2008) (released after his death) was a critical and popular success. But his biggest contribution to pop culture may have been his portrayal of homosexual cowboy Ennis Del Mar, living in the closet for decades while secretly yearning for a life with his first male lover, Jack Twist, in the movie *Brokeback Mountain* (2005).

DECADE IN REVIEW

The 2000s started in fear, continued in fear, moved into hope, and progressed to disillusionment. But through it all, Americans found icons and trailblazers—sometimes in unlikely places—who contributed immeasurably to popular culture in the new millennium.

Where will it all go as the millennium continues? It's anyone's guess. All the last six decades have shown us is that icons can come from the most unlikely places, and their lives can be long and fruitful or short and tragic. Either way, they gain the attention of the American public and leave an indelible mark on popular culture for future generations.

Notes

CHAPTER 1

p. 15–16, "I understand when I ... eighteen months." Wigg, David. "My Husband Picked Up the Phone and I Said, 'I Know You're in Bed with Liz Taylor': Debbie Reynolds on the Pain of Losing Her Husband." *Daily Mail*, April 23, 2010. http://www.dailymail.co.uk/tvshowbiz/article-1268158/Debbie-Reynolds-losing-husband-Eddie-Fisher-Elizabeth-Taylor.html#ixzz3tlIqS100.

p. 22, Lyrics of "American Pie." McLean, Don. www.azlyrics.com/lyrics/donmclean/americanpie.html.

CHAPTER 2

p. 23, "Don't let it be ... Camelot again." Pierson, James. "How Jackie Kennedy Invented the Camelot Legend After JFK's Death." *Daily Beast*, November 12, 2013. http://www.thedailybeast.com/articles/2013/11/12/how-jackie-kennedy-invented-the-camelot-legend-after-jfk-s-death.html.

p. 26, "one of the greatest style icons of the last century." "In Photos: Jackie Kennedy Onassis's Iconic Style." *Harper's Bazaar*. http://www.harpersbazaar.com/fashion/trends/g1370/jackie-kennedy-onassis-style-0111.

p. 28, Lyrics of "Blowin' in the Wind." Dylan, Bob. www.bobdylan.com/us/songs/blowin-wind.

p. 30, Lyrics of "Imagine." Lennon, John. www.azlyrics.com/lyrics/johnlennon/imagine.html.

p. 32, "more popular than Jesus." "John Lennon: 'We're More Popular Than Jesus.'" Beatles Bible. http://www.beatlesbible.com/1966/03/04/how-does-a-beatle-live-by-maureen-cleave.
p. 33, "he must have the constitution of an ox." "Who, What, Why: How Is Keith Richards Still Alive?" BBC.com, October 28. 2010. http://www.bbc.com/news/magazine-11621076.
p. 34, "the greatest instrumentalist in the history of rock music." The Jimi Hendrix Experience Biography. Rock and Roll Hall of Fame and Museum. http://rockhall.com/inductees/the-jimi-hendrix-experience/bio.
p. 36, "working man's ... Monroe." Nelson, Andrew. "Jayne Mansfield: The Brand Called Two." *Salon*, August 6, 2001. http://www.salon.com/2001/08/06/jayne_mansfield.

CHAPTER 3

p. 40, "the luxury ... of dwelling upon the self." Wolfe, Tom. "The 'Me' Decade and the Third Great Awakening." *New York*, August 23, 1976. http://nymag.com/news/features/45938.
p. 44, "pioneers of dance-oriented pop." Bee Gees. Rock and Roll Hall of Fame Museum. http://web.archive.org/web/20050616181341/http://www.rockhall.com/hof/inductee.asp?id=66.

CHAPTER 6

p. 80, "It destroyed me ... you're hated." "Ellen DeGeneres on 20/20." ABC News. http://abcnews.go.com/2020/story?id=124308&page=1.

Glossary

blacklist A group of people viewed negatively or with suspicion.

Black Nationalism A movement promoting separatism for black Americans.

bombshell An extremely attractive female.

civil disobedience Peaceful political protest.

civil rights A movement to ensure equal opportunity and privilege for African Americans.

Cold War An era of political tension and hostility between the United States and its allies and the Soviet Union and its allies, usually thought to have lasted from about 1945 until 1990.

communist Describing a political system in which all property is collectively owned and society is essentially free from classes.

conspiracy theory A belief that an organization is secretly responsible for some particular circumstance or event.

counterculture People who espouse a set of values that are contrary to the established societal norms.

dowry Money or goods given to a husband or wife before marriage.

falsetto A very high singing voice.

feminist A person who believes that women should be equal to men in political, social, and economic matters.

genocide The systematic killing of a group of people, often for reasons based on politics, religion, or ethnicity.

hallucinogenic Inducing hallucinations, as a drug; LSD was a popular hallucinogenic drug in the 1960s.

hippie A member of the counterculture who appeared unconventional in his or her clothing and was often associated with drug culture and a rejection of long-held societal values.

impeachment The process of removing an elected official from office.

Islamism Based on the Islamic religion, Islamism is a political movement that encourages a fundamental return to the early tenets of Islam.

LGBT A collective group that includes the lesbian, gay, bisexual, and transgender communities.

paparazzi Freelance photographers who take pictures of celebrities and sell them to various publications and news outlets.

patriarchy A society controlled by males.

persona How someone is perceived by others.

philanthropist A person who donates money to good causes.

photojournalism A practice of using photography to convey news and current events.

platinum A designation given to a record when it sells over one million copies.

psychedelic A 1960s rock music genre that focuses on musical experimentation and often describes drug-related scenarios in the lyrics.

Rastafarian A member of a Jamaican religious movement that believes black people are the chosen ones.

suburbs The outlying residential areas of a city.

Further Information

BOOKS

Cohen, Andy. *Most Talkative: Stories from the Front Lines of Pop Culture*. New York: St. Martin's Griffin, 2013.

Epting, Chris. *Hello, It's Me: Dispatches from a Pop Culture Junkie*. Solana Beach, CA: Santa Monica Press, 2010.

Johnston, Robert K., Craig Detweiler, and Barry Taylor, eds. *Don't Stop Believin': Pop Culture and Religion from Ben-Hur to Zombies*. Louisville, KY: Westminster John Knox Press, 2012.

Mansour, David. *From ABBA to Zoom: A Pop Culture Encyclopedia of the Late 20th Century*. Kansas City, MO: Andrews McMeel Publishing, 2005.

Weiss, Brett. *Retro Pop Culture A to Z: From Atari 2600 to Zombie Films*. CreateSpace Independent Publishing Platform, 2014.

FILMS

Grease. Warner Bros. Home Video, 1978.

How to Marry a Millionaire. Twentieth Century Fox Home Entertainment, 1953.

Mrs. Doubtfire. Twentieth Century Fox, 1993.

Star Wars Episode IV: A New Hope. Lucasfilm, 1977.

WEBSITES

Huff Post Celebrities
www.huffingtonpost.com/news/celebrities
Huff Po is an online news and blog site that began as a liberal news site but has since expanded into multiple areas beyond news and now features quite a robust section on celebrities.

Mr. PopCulture
www.mrpopculture.com
This website contains easy-to-follow links to each year so users can browse through what was popular in any given year.

People
www.people.com
People began as a print magazine about pop culture and still exists in that form, but it has expanded into a strong web presence as well. If there is reliable news to be had about celebrities, People.com will have it. Search for your favorite pop icons to learn more.

Bibliography

Allen, Joe. "When Lucy Was a Red." SocialistWorker.org, August 11, 2011. http://socialistworker.org/2011/08/11/when-lucy-was-a-red.

"Bee Gees." Rock and Roll Hall of Fame Museum. http://web.archive.org/web/20050616181341/http://www.rockhall.com/hof/inductee.asp?id=66.

Couch, Aaron. "'Saturday Night Live' Stars Who Died Before Their Time." *Hollywood Reporter*, October 9, 2014. http://www.hollywoodreporter.com/gallery/saturday-night-live-stars-who-739733/10-next-gallery.

"Elvis Presley." PBS.org. http://www.pbs.org/wgbh/cultureshock/flashpoints/music/elvis.html.

Gower, Eleanor. "The Half-Million Dollar Dress, $400,000 Venue and $7,000 7ft Cake: How Kim Kardashian and Kanye West Splashed Out $12 Million on Their Lavish Wedding." *Daily Mail*, May 28, 2014. http://www.dailymail.co.uk/tvshowbiz/article-2641836/The-half-million-dollar-dress-410-000-venue-7-000-cake-How-Kim-Kardashian-Kanye-West-splashed-12-million-lavish-wedding.html.

Handy, Bruce. "Music: Never Mind." *Time*, April 18, 1994. http://content.time.com/time/magazine/article/0,9171,980562,00.html.

Harrison, Scott. "Lucille Ball Explains 1936 Communist Link." *Los Angeles Times*, September 15, 2011. http://framework.latimes.com/2011/09/15/lucille-ball-explains-1936-communist-link.

"Harry Potter Finale Sales Hit 11m." BBC News, July 23, 2007. http://news.bbc.co.uk/2/hi/entertainment/6912529.stm.

"In Photos: Jackie Kennedy Onassis's Iconic Style." *Harper's Bazaar*. http://www.harpersbazaar.com/fashion/trends/g1370/jackie-kennedy-onassis-style-0111/.

"The Jimi Hendrix Experience Biography." Rock and Roll Hall of Fame and Museum. http://rockhall.com/inductees/the-jimi-hendrix-experience/bio/.

"Keeping Up with the Kardashians and Their Net Worth." *Huffington Post*, August 21, 2015. http://www.huffingtonpost.com/moneytips/keeping-up-with-the-karda_1_b_8014622.html.

Klosterman, Chuck. "'Taylor Swift on 'Bad Blood,' Kanye West, and How People Interpret Her Lyrics." *GQ*, October 15, 2015. http://www.gq.com/story/taylor-swift-gq-cover-story.

Levy, Shawn. "Dark Heart of Mr Sundance: A New Book Claims Hollywood's Golden Boy Paul Newman Was a Drunken Philanderer." *Daily Mail*, May 1, 2009. http://www.dailymail.co.uk/tvshowbiz/article-1176388/Dark-heart-Mr-Sundance-A-new-book-claims-Hollywoods-golden-boy-Paul-Newman-drunken-philanderer.html.

Montgomery, James. "Nirvana's *Nevermind*, by the Numbers." MTV News, September 23, 2011. http://www.mtv.com/news/1671298/nevermind-nirvana-album/.

Sessums, Kevin. "Elizabeth Taylor Interview About Her AIDS Advocacy." *Daily Beast*, March 23, 2011. http://www.thedailybeast.com/articles/2011/03/23/elizabeth-taylor-interview-about-her-aids-advocacy-plus-stars-remember.html.

Shinkman, Paul D. "Obama: 'Global War on Terror' Is Over." *U.S. News & World Report*, May 23, 2013. http://www.usnews.com/news/articles/2013/05/23/obama-global-war-on-terror-is-over.

"Top 10 Mistresses." *Time*. http://content.time.com/time/specials/packages/article/0,28804,1908008_1908007_1907992,00.html.

Weisman, Aly. "J.K. Rowling Is No Longer a Billionaire, Booted Off Forbes List." *Business Insider*, March 12, 2012. http://www.businessinsider.com/jk-rowling-is-no-longer-a-billionaire-booted-off-forbes-list-2012-3.

Willman, Chris. "Taylor Swift Tapes VH1 'Storytellers,' Lifts Curtain on New Songs from 'Red.'" *Hollywood Reporter*, October 17, 2012. http://www.hollywoodreporter.com/news/taylor-swift-tapes-vh1-storytellers-379446.

"Women and Work After World War II." PBS.org. http://www.pbs.org/wgbh/americanexperience/features/general-article/tupperware-work/.

Zara, Christopher. "'SNL' Dead Cast Members: Amid 40th Celebration, a List of 'Saturday Night Live' Players Who Went Too Soon." *International Business Times*, February 14, 2015. http://www.ibtimes.com/snl-dead-cast-members-amid-40th-celebration-list-saturday-night-live-players-who-went-1816398.

Index

Page numbers in **boldface** are illustrations. Entries in **boldface** are glossary terms.

About the Author

CATHLEEN SMALL is an author and editor who has written numerous books for Cavendish Square Publishing. A voracious reader, Cathleen has a keen interest in pop culture, particularly from the 1980s to the present. Cathleen lives in the San Francisco Bay Area with her two young sons and too many animals.